THE CRY OF A GENERATION
When Torn-mentors; Become Tormentors

Lawrence James Moore, Jr.

THE CRY OF A GENERATION

When Torn-mentors; Become Tormentors

Lawrence James Moore, Jr.

The Cry of A Generation: When Torn-mentors Become Tormentors
By Lawrence James Moore, Jr.

Millennial Enterprise & Publishing Co'
Email: pastormoore86@gmail.com

This book or parts thereof may not be reproduce in any form, stored in a retrieval system, or transformed in any form by any means-electronic, mechanical, photocopy, recording or otherwise- without permission of the Author or Publisher, except as provided by the United States of America copyright Law.

Unless otherwise noted, all Scriptures quotation are from the KING JAMES VERSION of the Bible.

ISBN: 978-1-945377-01-3

Copyright © Revised 2017 by Lawrence James Moore, Jr
All rights reserved.

Acknowledgements

I would like to thank God; He has been my inspiration through my most difficult moments. I would also like to thank my four daughters: Lauren, Shekinah, Amya and Lauriyana my loves and angels who pushed me without even knowing they did. I also would like to thank my son Mekhi, whom I am constantly reminded is one of the reasons I was inspired to write this book.

I thank my mother, Mary Moore, who has been a great mother. Bishop Tommy Reid, I love and appreciate you. I also would like to give thanks my wife Ayanna Moore who labors with me.

Foreword

The Cry of a Generation is a book whose time has come. Author Lawrence James Moore, Jr. addresses the problems of our cities and churches and the answer that God provides through Christ and his Kingdom. This talented author, pastor, teacher, and leader knows what he is writing about. Brought up on the streets of a decaying urban city, he first expressed the genius of his leadership as founder of W.B. (Walden Boys), which is a local street gang in the city Buffalo. After spending the majority of his late teens and early adult life in prison, Lawrence experienced an encounter with Christ shortly after his release.

I first met Lawrence as a student in one of my classes at the famed Elim Bible Institute, where he was a student studying for Christian ministry. I was immediately impressed with his keen intellect as well as his potential leadership abilities. It was not long after my encounter with Lawrence that he opened a church in the inner city of Buffalo. This church was located in one of the most dangerous areas of our city. It was here that I watched this "leader of men" begin to emerge as a successful pastor. It was not without great difficulty. He began to build a church in a venue where most of the residents are virtually suffering because of drugs, gang violence, and unemployment. The church was soon full of people worshipping God and listening to this man expound the Word of God. Eventually he moved the church to a location where there was adequate parking and space for vital service programs to serve our city.

As this leader began to emerge and his ministry became more

effective, he sat down and wrote this manuscript. It is the observation of one who has not studied this topic from a classroom, but one who grew up in the very city where leadership is continually decaying. This is where God has called him to minister. He knows the problems and he knows the answer. He also realizes the problem that exists in leadership, thus the subtitle of the book, *When Torn-mentors Become Tormentors*. Leaders who are themselves troubled cannot meet the needs of the people or their cities.

I suggest that you read with an open mind the words of a man who first "was the problem," and secondly came to "bring an answer to the problem." In addressing the problem himself, he began to see the flaws in contemporary leadership and the church of the twenty- first century. This book is the observations of one who knows. We are all learners and pilgrims in a difficult world. I ask you to hear with your heart the cry of a young apostle of God who has a passion for the cities of the world.

Senior Pastor Tommy Reid
The Tabernacle
Orchard Park, New York

Preface

Pastor Moore's *The Cry of A Generation: When Torn-mentors Become Tormentors* is a powerful reminder of the role of the mentor and desperate need of the mentee for qualified mentorship. His message is one that is timeless, cross-generational and an imperative announcement for today's twenty-first century church and modern day generation

The sound of the cry of this generation's youth, and succeeding leadership for instruction, advisement and coaching, is one whose frequency would seemingly and all too often render it audible to only the observant, and those in need. In this impeccably timed announcement, Moore brings the sound of this incessant cry for help within the hearing range of "all," allowing the hurt and damaged preceding leaders of all walks to see the tormenting effects of their past and present emotional and mental dilemmas passed on through the mentoring of tomorrow's leaders.

The Cry of A Generation: When Torn-mentors Become Tormentors reminds us that the destructive forces in our world—amongst our families and youth, socio-economical, criminal, and most imperatively "spiritual"—are not the result of a generation simply gone recklessly astray. A great deal is the direct result of our own disconnect with our responsibility as leaders via parental-leadership, social-leadership, youth-leadership, and critically imperative spiritual-Leadership to understand and embrace the "mentoring" responsibility.

Moore remarkably points out to us that successful leadership in any capacity is not complete simply because one was successful to his or her leadership cause, but as demonstrated by Elijah to Elisha, successful leadership is only complete when any leader carefully and strategically considers tomorrow, and leaves a legacy of hope for a future generation.

Pastor Quincy Baker
Greater New Life Worship Center, Inc. Buffalo, New York

Contents

INTRODUCTION 11

CHAPTER 1: The Cry of a Generation. 13

CHAPTER 2: The Torn-Mentor..39

CHAPTER 3: When the Torn-Mentor Mentors: The Law of Transference and Reproduction 59

CHAPTER 4: Refusing To Carry It Over" 75

CHAPTER 5: Forgive, Forget and "Move Forward 99

CHAPTER 6: Mentoring After the Father's Heart 115

CHAPTER 7: Giving Generations What They Need. 135

CHAPTER 8: Be Careful "Who" You Chase 153

CHAPTER 9: The Great Mentor 169

CHAPTER 10: Ready for the Impartation. 185

ABOUT THE AUTHOR..199

Introduction

The Cry of A Generation: When Torn-mentors Become Tormentors is a book that targets the lack of mentoring both in our society and in the Christian church. The content is three-dimensional: first, the book is one of awareness; second, it is a book of healing; and third, it points those who are in search of mentoring in the direction of Christ. This book is written to help you reach beyond the pain of your past and move beyond the pain of your present and, despite the tormentors of your life, realize that the cry of your heart has been heard in Heaven. The answer that God sent is in Jesus Christ the Messiah. This book will help you discover the purpose behind your pain and give you the inner healing that you need to be an effective Kingdom witness, and walk in the power and authority that you were designed to walk in.

The Cry of A Generation: When Torn-mentors Become Tormentors, was written as a mandate to carry out the first commission of every believer whose call is to bring healing and restoration to the Body of Christ, according to Matthew 10:6-8a: *"But go rather to the lost sheep of the house of Israel. And as ye go, preach, saying. The kingdom of heaven is at hand. Heal the sick, cleanse the lepers, raise the dead, cast out devils."* Our first call and commission is to the church, the body of Christ; for, if it's not healed and restored, how can we heal and restore the world? *The Cry of a Generation: When Tormentors Becomes Torn-Mentors* is both an answer to a cry and a prophetic voice for what God is doing in the twenty-first century church. The Kingdom of God and the world is depending on YOU, so take this journey as your road to healing. Your complete restoration begins now. Even though this book has multiple chapters, its entire content is the beginning of a new chapter in your life.

Chapter One
The Cry of a Generation

There are many ways I could have chosen to approach this book and subject of "mentoring." I feel the most fitting way, however, is to recognize and pinpoint the need and "cry of this generation." If we were to bring our ears closer to the sound of the matter, we would hear that this generation suffers from a severe lack of mentors—a responsibility that bears more weight than one may initially realize. The responsibility to mentor is the responsibility to empower the next generation. Since the next generation of any imperative brings completeness to its predecessors, in some sense the responsibility of mentoring not only leaves a legacy behind, but brings completeness to all of those who assume this great responsibility. Our greatest leadership contributions are far from complete without leaving a legacy of hope through the generations that succeed us.

When I received the mandate to write this book, it was based on the critical need to address the lack of mentors for our next generation of boys, teens, and young men. A closer look at the incalculability of this dilemma, however, has forced my eyes open and has pressed me to speak to the general population—male, female, young, and old. All of us are a part of the mentoring process whether as mentors or mentees. The future leadership of our society and the imperative, "God's Kingdom," is desperately crying for mentorship. We can see how deeply this generation suffers from the lack of men- tors, both naturally and spiritually, through a simple routine look at the evening news, or by stepping outside our homes, or by driving to and from work. At any selected moment we are incessantly reminded of the relentless cries for "the mentor."

IDENTIFYING THE MENTOR

Who is the mentor? What does he or she look like? When I consider the responsibility of mentoring, I consider it is worth mentioning that the responsibility of mentoring crosses multiple levels. Parents and mentors, for example, take on very similar responsibilities. The mere presence of parents in a house no more supposes they are assuming their parental-mentoring responsibilities than does their mere presence alone guarantee that a house is a "home." Crime rates continue to increase due to a lack of mentors and parental- mentoring.

As for the spiritual mentor, a closer look at today's young leaders of the Body of Christ reveals the need for more proper spiritual mentoring. This is not just the chronological leader via age, but even the spiritual leader who encounters shipwreck in a ministry that runs rampant with sin and rebellion because the Body of

Christ ("The Church") has not "maximized" its mentoring position and responsibility. Concerning the "where" of the matter let me also say that the concern is not an urban or a suburban issue, but a Kingdom dilemma. Our lack of mentoring amongst our spiritual leaders exists in part, because generations before were not aware of the imperativeness of the responsibility to mentor and the depth of the potential impact that could result without it. Our society and religious communities are filled with people who are overly preoccupied with themselves and not aware and connected enough to tomorrow. Even our connection to the responsibility of mentorship with regard to family roles has greatly diminished. We live in a self-centered society where sin and rebellion is overpowering even the church. From the pulpits to the pews, this religious compromise has birthed mentors who are too busy seeking greatness—mentors who are bound by traditions, organizations, position, power, and prestige—ultimately blinding them from preparing a future generation. They themselves lack the moral values required to prepare the upcoming generations that are "crying" behind them. Like a dog whistle, the cries ring at a certain amplitude and in a spiritual, emotional and mental frequency range that only the spiritually- minded, experienced, trained ear can hear.

Nonetheless, make no mistake about it, in the absence of our own focus, "mentors are always there." Our city streets are dominated by boys and young men who are being mentored by gang leaders, drug dealers, and playboys. They lurk in corners waiting to jump out and seize an opportunity to mentor or torment the available mentee; running interference on the mature, successful men and women—Christian and non-Christian alike—who have a sense of direction and insistency to put others on similar paths to help them identify their own course of direction. Even the leaders in our churches have been affected by these pseudo-mentors who have been unveiled as pimps, playboys, pedophiles, abusive, domineering men and women without restraint. I believe this is an obvious result of a lack of concern on the part of the leaders in our society and Christian community. We lack the tools required to mentor because the leaders that have gone before us have not passed the tools on to the future generations. In addition, their own micro- Kingdom has become their main focus, and has left them concerned only about producing people who can manage and maintain their own empires and traditions. They long to control instead of leading men and women, and capturing the hearts of a lost generation.

So what do solutions to this generational epidemic look like? I believe that "the believer" is the key to changing our world and our society. The Church and the believer have always been divinely responsible to "go first"—placed in our communities to be bright lights and examples that refuse to go silently into the night. Deuteronomy 6:6-9 states:

And these words, which I command you this day, shall be in your heart: And you shall teach them diligently to your children, and shalt talk of them when you sit in thine house, and when you walk by the way, and when you lay down, and when you rise up. And thou shalt bind them for a sign upon thine hand, and they shall be as frontlets between thine eyes. And thou shalt write them upon the posts of thy house, and on thy gates.

These are instructions that God spoke to the leader Moses, which he gave to the children of Israel as a road map to instruct them and their children. But there is a cry in the earth for something that exceeds instruction alone. This generation cries for someone to "show" them how to live God's word or to live life by example; to show them how to be accepted and respected by God. The advertisements and commercial are nice, but this generation is looking for a demonstration and working floor model of the product we pro- pose in our social and religious instruction. Who will stand up and show me the model mentor? It is worth noting at this point that to instruct someone requires far less time and effort than mentoring.

The problem with the first family (Adam and Eve) did not occur as a result of lack of instruction, because we know that Adam as God's first man was well instructed. But Adam's own instructions to his family were not followed through with conviction at a pivotal time when his "example" would matter the most. Eve's response to the serpent proves she was well instructed. She had read the manual but was lacking in mentorship-by-example—someone (Adam) to show her how (a proper usage of the information) it worked. As we all know, whenever we mentor or raise children, they seem to rarely do what we say or instruct them to do. More often (and often at the wrong times), they follow after our examples because children are ever learning and have not put in the time on the job to develop a total comprehension of what's really before them. In the meantime, it's on-the-job training for them—they follow our example until what begins as mere mimicry eventually turns into understanding and self-awareness.

Adam accepted something that he should have rejected according to the instructions that God had given him. In addition, instead of repenting for his disobedience, he tried to hide and cover it up. The first step to restoring the mentor is to acknowledge our failure to provide proper mentoring. We must take ownership for what we have (or should I say have not) produced. God's instructions to Adam in Genesis 2:16-17, were the following: *"And the Lord God commanded the man, saying, Of every tree of the garden thou mayest freely eat. But of the tree of the knowledge of good and evil, thou shalt not eat of it: for in the day that thou eat thereof thou shalt surely die."*

Let's consider for a moment Cain, Adam's eldest son, as our next mentee by example. As with Eve, his struggle was the result of what his father did not do. As mentors, what "we" do will have a greater impact on future generations than we think. Abel's offering was accepted, or respected—he had no need for repentance. Cain's was not and in his cry for acceptance and for someone to show him how to repent, he became angry and killed his brother. This is what I believe happened; let us read what the Word says.

And in process of time it came to pass, that Cain brought

of the fruit of the ground an offering unto the Lord. And Abel, he also brought of the firstlings of his flock and of the fat thereof. And the Lord had respect unto Abel and to his offering: But unto Cain and to his offering he had not respect. And Cain was very wroth, and his countenance fell. And the LORD said unto Cain, Why art thou wroth? and why is thy countenance fallen? If thou doest well, shalt thou not be accepted? and if thou doest not well, sin lieth at the door. And unto thee shall be his desire, and thou shalt rule over him. And Cain talked with Abel his brother: and it came to pass, when they were in the field, that Cain rose up against Abel his brother, and slew him.
—*Genesis 4:3-8*

The first thing you must recognize is that Cain's offering was a second hand offering, while Abel's was of the firstling of the flock. Let's take a closer look at the word respect. Paying careful attention to its Hebrew origin, in its primitive root meaning it is defined as to gaze at or about, by implication to inspect or consider. Now we know that God requires more than just a proper offering; He requires the correct attitude as well. The Bible lets us know that God had respect unto Abel and his offering, but unto Cain and his offering He had not respect. Because of Abel's attitude in his giving, coupled with the fact that he brought to God what he desired (an offering of the firstlings of the flock or a blood offering), God considered, inspected, and received it. On the other hand, because Cain's offering was a second-hand offering and his attitude in giving it was improper, God neither considered, gazed at, nor inspected it. God provided Cain space for repentance, but his failure to comply with God's offer (to repent) was the result of his father's (Cain's parental-mentor) failure to repent. Why don't apples fall far from trees? This is called the law of reproduction, a topic we will deal with in more detail later. The point I wanted to make is simply to show that Adam's failure as the first man, father and parental-mentor, caused him to release, seminally, failure in his off- spring. His failure to lead by example became the torment of another generation.

SEEKING THE MENTOR AND TRUSTING THE "RIGHT ONE"

First John 4:1 states, "Beloved, believe not every spirit, but try the spirits whether they are of God: because many false prophets are gone out into the world." The word believe is the key word in this text. It means to have faith in, upon, or with respect to, a person or thing. By implication it means to entrust, especially one's spiritual well-being, to Christ; to commit to trust, put in trust with. This is a warning, a "beware of the dog sign" as it relates to the person seeking someone to mentor them. You cannot commit to trust your life and purpose with just anyone, he or she must be "worthy" and "trustworthy" of the trust with which you give them. While considering who will be entrusted with the responsibility of mentoring, it is important that as a mentee, you have faith and entrust your spiritual well-being first to Christ. The word believe comes from the word faith, which means persuasion, credence; moral conviction of religious truth, or the truthfulness of God or a religious teacher, especially reliance upon Christ for salvation.

So the question that lingers in the minds of people seeking mentoring is, how do I know I've found the right one? Sounds like we're about to pop the million-dollar question, right? Believe you me, selecting a mentor is a sacred decision. Well, my answer to you is based upon the Word of God: ...*Try the spirit...*" because "*...when he, the Spirit of truth, is come, he will guide you into all truth: for he shall not speak of himself; but whatsoever he shall hear, that shall he speak: and he will show you things to come.* John 16:13 has made this step in the process self-explanatory. The mentee must be spiritually in tune and aware to discern the spirit of his or her mentor. The mentee must possess an internal "level" that enables him or her to see a prospective mentor is indeed aligned (or level) with God's will. If your mentor has the wrong spirit, this could very well be the beginning of a mentor that will not mentor, but torment you.

COMPATIBILITY AND THE ROLES OF THE MENTOR

The role of the mentor is three-dimensional. A mentor is a wise advisor, teacher, and coach. A mentor is one who imparts life by way of action and instruction. A mentor is sort of a forerunner for the person he or she is mentoring. To be a mentor means not only that you impart life, but there is also a transference of life from one vessel to another. Mentoring is a joint effort on behalf of the mentor and the mentee. As a mentor, you have to be discerning because you cannot mentor everyone that desires you to mentor them—mentoring necessitates "chemistry." There is a certain harmony and connection that must be in place. The mentee must be willing to submit to your counsel, accept your advice as his or her advisor, accept your correction as a teacher, and be coached through both his or her life's failures and successes. As the mentee, you must understand that just because you long for mentoring or just because a given person appeals to you, and may even have characteristics similar to your own, this does not guarantee chemistry. Characteristic and personality traits mean a lot. The pieces must fit together as perfectly as a puzzle piece, into the shape that has been cut for only that individual piece.

> Oftentimes, up-and-coming mentees spend too much time chasing behind men and women of God, or other people they desire to be mentored by, but who are neither called to you, sent nor ordained of God. Although they appear to have a great deal of gifts and anointing with them, they may not possess or be willing to provide the time, patience, attitude or Kingdom traits consistent with what God desires to produce in you. This is why a mentor has to be one who is sent, not one who merely arrives or is hastily selected. He or she must have the ability to see beyond where you are as the mentee and possess a third eye, to see your potential not just to succeed, but to also push and encourage you to exceed even "them- selves." This is the role and compatibility of the true mentor. We're only in the beginning of our discussion, and by now you are already reconsidering the roles of persons in your life who you thought held mentoring potential. Or perhaps you are wondering about the potential of others who until now, you may not have

considered mentors. If I am challenging you to mentally, spiritually and emotionally think then I am already beginning to achieve my goal. But keep your hands in until the ride comes to a complete stop: there is much more to be considered about your future as a mentee and ultimate destiny as a mentor.

THE ADVISOR

As earlier mentioned, what qualifies a good mentor, besides having the spirit is his or her ability to advise, teach, and coach well. As an advisor, the mentor is to give advice to, to counsel, to offer as advice; to notify or inform, to be a counselor; to instruct or to be a consultant. The Hebrew word for advice is a primitive root meaning to deliberate or resolve, and advertise. To deliberate means to carefully think out, not rashly, hastily or hurriedly, but to consider carefully. The mentor is a patient teacher, expecting the mentee to make mistakes and to not fully grasp all that is being taught "immediately." To resolve is to break in separate parts, to change or to solve a problem; to breakdown challenges to the mentee into less overwhelming and more manageable chunks. To advise means to describe or praise publicly, usually so as to promote—this adds heightened value to the role as advisor or counselor. Although all three roles are necessary, you cannot have good teachers and coaches in your life without the balance of a good advisor. A good advisor counsels you carefully through difficult periods in your life, helping to correct your errors with precise patience. They are not in a rush to push you off to premature success lest an additional shipwreck is encountered. The advisor knows how to bring announcement to and build platforms for "you." Good counsel, correction, and promotion are what this generation desperately needs and is crying for.

To go a little deeper, when we speak about promotion we are really speaking of the type of elevation that comes even from correction. Proverbs 11:14 states: *"Where no counsel is, the people fall: but in the multitude of counsellors there is safety."* Proverbs 15:22 states: *"Without counsel purposes are disappointed: but in the multitude of counselors they are established."* And my last scriptural reference is Proverbs 20:18, which states, *"Every purpose is established by counsel: and with good advice make war."*

As we know from biblical history, the men and women of God who made excellent advisors or counselors where those who heard from God, and advised after the Father's heart. Purpose was established, destiny was pursued, and war under good advice and counsel was sought before and after victory. A mentor that advises well has the ability to promote your spiritual and natural lives, or demote and destroy both. Oh, what a delight it would be to know that your life is in the care of a man or woman whose life is in God's hand. All too often, the mentored is too immature to hear God's voice distinctively. I suggest to you that God will use a "Terah" who will hear God concerning you, while simultaneously working to bring you to the place of maturity where you, as the mentee, can hear God for yourself. This brings you closer to the transition from mentee to mentor. Just some food for thought: let us consider what

Genesis 11:31-32 states: *And Terah took Abram his son, and Lot the son of Haran his son's son, and Sarai his daughter-in-law, his son Abram's wife; and they went forth with him from Ur of the Chaldees, to go into the land of Canaan; and they came unto Haran, and dwelt there. And the days of Terah were two hundred and five years: and Terah died in Haran.*

Notice, God did not speak to Abram directly at first, probably because of immaturity. Instead, he speaks to his father, who was also his mentor, advisor, teacher, and coach. He speaks to Terah in Ur of the Chaldees, a wealthy populous and sophisticated, pagan center of Southern Mesopotamia. (The name Ur meant flame or fire, and referred to the fire of God's judgment.) Then he tells Terah to move to Haran, which means parched. Parch means to make hot and dry; to make very thirsty. Listen to this: Terah brings Abram from a place which was about to catch God's judgment, to a place of thirstiness, and then dies. Advice from a good advisor will bring you to the point of safety in proper thirst, while simultaneously moving you out of harm's way.

In Abram's dryness or thirstiness God speaks to him, and says in Genesis 12:1: *"Now the Lord had said unto Abram, Get thee out of thy country, and from thy kindred, and from thy father's house, unto a land that I will show thee."* Only after he was promoted to the place of maturity, did his father act as his advisor, making sure that he deliberated the plans of God for Abram. He resolved the up-and coming problem by moving him out of harm's way, and promoted him to the place of maturity—the place where he can now hear

God for "himself." This is the role of a mentor as an advisor: to hear the plans of God for the mentee. When, because of spiritual immaturity, you are unable to hear God's voice, the critical question is, "Can your mentor hear for you?" Your mentor's advice should lead to elevation and promotion, not aggravation and demotion. When a tormentor advises you, their advice tends to lead to a tare in your mental and emotional peace and stability, and throws your purpose and destiny completely of course. Bad advice is always the reason why most people's lives end up in shipwreck. You can never recover time lost from being wrongly advised; but you can prevent it by not being extremely anxious and by allowing God to spiritually redeem that which has been lost by accepting the proper mentor or, as the mentor, by redefining your own mentoring approach.

THE TEACHER: THE TORMENT OF NEEDING INSTRUCTION

My torment began with my own seeking to be taught. I was raised in a predominately female household. I was taught how to cook and clean, but deep inside I felt there was more in me to be produced. Constant engagement in even childlike play with girls produced a feeling of disconnect or a gap, amplifying the cry within me for instruction. I had four younger brothers whom I tormented as children with youthful bullying. Where this came from I cannot tell you, but what it led to was far worse than my incomplete upbringing. I began to look to the streets for someone to teach me to be anything that produced some kind of purpose because I did not know who I was, or what I wanted be. The streets became my men- tor, my teacher. During this time, I picked up a lot of weights and sins that halted anything my mother had properly instilled within me through parental-mentoring and family Bible studies each night. Every mentor must have the ability to teach

In addition to this generation's cry for a working model, there is yet the cry for someone to "teach and instruct us so we can be accepted." It's sad to long to be taught and educated, and your cries go unheard, especially when your life depends on it. The lack of knowledge on any level is the reason why generation after generation are perishing to false self-awareness. To a desperate generation, improper teachings have the potential to be pursued after and learned wrongly. Teaching must be properly "used" and not improperly "abused." To teach means to provide knowledge or insight; to show or help a person to learn how to do something. I have seldom been advantaged with the opportunities of great moments of instruction, instead I have more often been left to haphazardly discover who I am little by little, feeling my way in the dark while could-be-mentors shined there flashlights on their own agendas. I was never taught to discover who I was in life—I had to learn and discover through much difficulty and trial and error, who I was. I was never taught ministry or how to properly serve God, and I know without question that I have tormented others in the process of learning who I was. When a mentor fails to properly teach and instruct, it leads to great misunderstanding.

The Hebrew meaning of the word teaches or teacher means to bring or one who brings to another level of revelation. I like dealing with Greek and Hebrew because they always provide us with the primitive root (or original meaning of words) so you can understand their full meaning. In the Hebrew tongue, the word for teacher means properly to flow as water; to rain, to lay or throw, especially an arrow (to shoot). Figuratively, it means to point out (as by aiming the finger). So in one aspect a teacher is one who waters down, therefore nourishing the instilled knowledge, causing growth. The teacher also lays a foundation of knowledge, wisdom and under- standing, aiming or pointing you in the right direction for your purpose. A person who is not properly taught cannot properly lead. Is your life being watered down by the nourishing of the word of God? Or are you the victim of a tormentor who is watering your life down with their own disappointments, perceptions, bitterness, and anger from their tormented past? Some teachers will instruct you to despise things that they despise, or see things the way they see them—through the lenses of their own negative experiences. The effect is as if you were looking through someone else's glasses, and "you" yourself don't even wear them. Ouch! Now that's a big blur!

Therefore shall ye lay up these my words in your heart and in your soul, and bind them for a sign upon your hand, that they may be as frontlets between your eyes. And ye shall teach them your children, speaking of them when thou sittest in thine house, and when thou walkest by the way, when thou liest down, and when thou risest up. And thou shalt write them upon the door posts of thine house, and upon thy gates: that your days may be multiplied, and the days of your children, in the land which the LORD sware unto your fathers

to give them, as the days of heaven upon the earth.
—Deuteronomy 11:18-21

Do you know how many generations of teachers have read this but missed it? The teacher trait of the mentor is multiplication. As teachers in the Kingdom, we are to point those we mentor in the direction of Christ, not in the direction of our own personal agendas. This is the role of a teacher.

SET THE MARK!

When you combine the advisor and the teacher trait of the mentor, you are exercising Hebrews 12:1-2a, which says *Wherefore seeing we also are compassed about with so great a cloud of witnesses, let us lay aside every weight and the sin which doth so easily beset us, and let us run with patience the race that is set before us, looking at Jesus the author and finisher of our faith.*

Weights and sin affect how well you run. Sin produces a halt in your movement (your purpose); weights slow the process down. As teachers, we should possess the ability to see the "set mark" of those we mentor or teach. We should see the potential sin and weights that lay ahead because we as mentors have already gone before them, ridding ourselves of our own encumbrances. This is a benefit of both the mentor and the mentee, because in the advising and teaching portions of your destiny, mentors correct the mistakes of the mentees by teaching them how to overcome what they overcame.

Mentors point the mentee in the right direction, teaching him or her to avoid familiar pit stops along the way, because everything for your purpose as a mentee is written out and has gone before you—YOUR MARK IS SET! You are about to walk out the course that is being pointed out with patience. Keep your focus on the author and finisher of your faith, who is Jesus Christ—the teacher is the "witness" to an incredible blessing in the success of the mentee.

On the contrary, it is only when a teacher's witness is compromised by past or present failures, and is lacking the witness of the model of achievements and accomplishments, that you may be looking at a mentor who has still not laid aside every weight and the sin that is besetting them. The result is Torn-Mentoring. They are teaching (pointing) you in the direction of failure, of an incomplete path that they have not trodden, leaving the road rough and uncomfortable for the mentee to travel on. The point I'm seeking to make is that a mentor that is a tormentor is not just one who only mentally, emotionally or even physically scars you, but also one who causes the great intangible damage of deprived instruction and bad example. For every generation that goes untaught, there is a subsequent generation that will not be taught, and a generation that will go unlearned. Even if taught, the question of "what's" being taught still remains. The streets and the unqualified people I encountered became my first tormentors. Then, after moving on to the church after a life of torment, thinking I was running to safety, my torment only took on another level. It's now your turn, let me trail blaze the way.

The writer of Hebrews 5:12 says: *"For when for the time ye ought to be teachers, ye have need that one teach you again which be the first principles of the oracles of God; and are become such as have need of milk, and not of strong meat."* I believed that once I got to the church (to "safety"), I could begin healing from my tormented past. Much to my dismay, I have never encountered hurt as so religiously executed by the people of the good old church. I eventually learned that there was a difference between "church people" and Kingdom of God people. Kingdom people taught things that pertained to the Kingdom of God, while church people taught things that pertained to church (not "the" Church, but to "church"). But there was still a difference in the hurt and torment I experienced in the church, because this hurt and torment was actually pointing me in the right direction, the direction of Christ. This, too, was turning me to my salvation. Kingdom teachers are to teach things that pertain to the Kingdom.

In summary, true mentors impart into people what they are. Proverbs 9:9 says, *"Give instruction to a wise man, and he will yet be wiser: teach a just man, and he will increase in learning."* But the trick, so to speak, is for the teacher to be a wise and just person in order to make men and women thirsty for the Kingdom and wise— increasing in Kingdom learning. The mentor is not to make the mentee thirsty for the mentor, nor is the mentor to be merely thirsty after his or her own agenda. This produces only torment. So as the teacher, the mentor is constantly spilling knowledge over into the mentored, flowing as rivers of living waters, raining and nourishing the life of the individual while at the same time shooting as an arrow, as an archer planting a mark or goal ahead for the mentored to make. The mentor sets the mark, pointing the mentee in the right direction. What the mentor teaches is always a determination, whether what he or she teaches are words of life that will lead to spiritual maturity and natural success, or words of death that will lead to spiritual and natural disasters.

There is always an impartation—the question is, of what? The best mentors teach according to Kingdom principles (the principles of multiplication and production) and cause generations to come to flourish through the power of God's word. *"For by me,"* God says, *thy days shall be multiplied, and the years of thy life shall be increased"* (Proverbs 9:11); but also by one your days are subtracted and the years of your life can be decreased. What power! Because I was not taught ministry, who I was becoming as a church leader was being built and developed upon a flawed character—I was a tormentor in the making. It was not until I embarked upon my pastoral call that I gained a personal insight of what a real mentor should look like. Becoming a pastor pushed me into deeper dimensions of prayer, worship, and studying of the life of Christ, the greatest mentor that ever lived. My pastoral call did not push me into theological seminary because there was a hunger in me that school could not satisfy.

With all due respect to some of the greatest theologians and scholarly minds that have made some of the most invaluable contributions to our faith, it remains true that even some of the worst tor- mentors possess Masters and Doctorate degrees. They possess Doctors of Theology and Masters of Divinity from the classrooms of college campuses. The hope is that students and parishioners are taught more than theology and mere doctrine, while behind closed doors in the sacred moment of the "mentoring process." The teaching trait is important because a person will teach whatever they are taught. They will point those they teach in the same direction; they will guide them in the same course of life they themselves have taken. They will in effect be reproducers of either effective mentoring or torn-mentoring.

Who we are today is a result of the life experiences taught by pastors, teachers of varying roles, mothers, fathers, family, friends, professors, etc.; but the choice is ours—when we come into the knowledge of the truth—to remain in or to come out of incorrect mentoring. All of us are, in some shape or form, teachers. I feel it important to ask my readers to understand that as I take my time to delve into the depths of this book, it is my objective to paint a foundational picture and positive outlook of what the true mentor looks like, so you can see and understand the difference between a mentor that mentors and one that torments.

THE COACH

The last trait of a mentor is that of a coach. To coach means to instruct or train alongside. What sticks out with me is the word train, which means to guide the mental and moral development of, to instruct as to make proficient; to make fit for, and to aim. Moral development is a necessity for the person being mentored because it teaches right and wrong. It's good conduct or character; training that makes one capable of distinguishing between right or wrong. The condition of the mind is very important. As a man thinks, so is he. As a coach, the mentor has to train the person he or she is mentoring to always think and pull out the best of every situation. Coaches help train and prepare for competition and battle. As a coach, the mentor has to recognize his or her own ability to be more than just a conqueror, thinking themselves beyond where they are. Much of professional athletic training involves mental conditioning than anything. Training athletes to outsmart their opponent, shaping attitude towards the end goal and the process of getting there. Your attitude will always determine your altitude. The proper mindset is most relevant for a person's achievements.

This generation has seen so many mentors and potential mentors defeated in the area of the mind by yielding to sin, because they are unable to overcome mental conflict. Whenever you shift to a different environment or lifestyle, the focus of your conflicts should shift also. Understanding that your conflicts are spiritual should eliminate operating in the flesh. Your mentor has to be a spiritual giant because of the mental conflicts arising from the Kingdom of darkness. *"For we wrestle not against flesh and blood, but against principalities, against powers, against the rulers of the darkness of this world, against spiritual wickedness in high places"* (Ephesians 6:12). These forces of darkness are so dramatic that if mentors themselves have not overcome them by the blood of the Lamb, they are waiting to be transformed from a mentor into a tormentor— hardly a respectable career. This is why the mentor has to overcome his or her own mental stress, frustrations, and conflict from emotional, spiritual, or even physical pain or damage. They themselves have had to be conditioned in order to provide conditioning. As mentors, we coach from our experiences, whether they are good or bad, whether we are bound or free. The truth is you are either a victim or victor of your experiences, and pass on either a victim's or victor's perspective to the mentee.

Proverbs 22:6 says: *"Train up a child in the way he should go: and when he is old, he will not depart from it."* Let's consider this text for a moment. The word train gets its idea from the original Hebrew word, which is a primitive root, including the idea to dedicate, as well as educate. "In the way he should go" can mean according to his way; the child's habits and interests. The coach must take into account his individuality and inclinations and be in keeping with his or her degree of physical and mental development. The meaning of the word "way" comes from another Hebrew word which means a road or a course of life. The Bible specifically states "in the way of the Lord" because there are some other ways you can train or coach.

There are at least four personality or character differences, which we will get into a little later, which the mentor who coaches will train from. The first is from the personality of man, which can be full of selfishness and pride, personal gain, selfish ambition and human failure. The second is the personality of sin, which is strictly evil. The third is the personality of the church, which is traditional, ritualistic, and religious. And last is the personality of the Kingdom, which are the Beatitudes and the Similitude's we find in Matthew 5. So, mental development is vital to the moral progression of a person. Many mentors lost their coaching ability or never had an ability to coach, because they have not overcome their childhood, teenage, young adult, or adult experiences. This is the reason why we are producing more tormentors than mentors. When you have mentors who are qualified but will not do, the mentors who are unqualified yet are willing will step in. What you end up with is what we've been producing—mentors who are tormentors— mentors who continue to shipwreck lives by coaching generations how to torment. The most mind massaging text I've read is Philippians 4:8. Paul states: *Finally, brethren, whatsoever things are true, whatsoever things are honest, whatsoever things are just, whatsoever things are pure, whatsoever things are lovely, whatsoever things are of good report; if there be any virtue, and if there be any praise, think on these things.*

THE THREE-DIMENSIONAL CHRIST

The greatest mentor that ever lived was Jesus Christ; He possessed all three traits of the mentor. As an advisor, He deliberated and resolved the gospel so that His students did not receive too much too soon. Yet as they progressed, they received what they needed for the next phase of their lives and development, while also resolving conflict that arose among them from time to time. As a teacher, the Bible says in Matthew 5:1-2a: *"And seeing the multitudes, he went up into a mountain: and when he was set, his disciples came unto him: and he opened his mouth and taught them,"* pointing them in the direction of successful living in the Kingdom, while at the same time acting as coach.

The Beatitudes and the Similitudes represent a set mark, a goal that every mentor and those that are being mentored should be aiming at. When you understand the Beatitudes on the Kingdom level, you understand them to be the character and personality that comes with the Kingdom lifestyle. They are exercises for conditioning the mental and moral development of man. Jesus, our perfect example of one who was very patient and who taught with authority, had the power to influence those He mentored.

So as we pursue excellence in the Kingdom, we must fashion ourselves around Christ so that the crying of this generation can stop. When a generation cries, they zaaq (zaw-ak), as the Hebrews would say. It's a shriek (from anguish or danger). It is a verb meaning to cry out, to exclaim, and to call. The primary activity implies that of crying out in pain or by reason of affliction. The verb signifies the action of calling on the Lord in a time of need, uttering sounds of sorrow, distress or alarm, issuing a summons for help. For the able mentors that are unwilling to rise up and advise, teach and coach us into a truly apostolic anointing like that which Jesus Christ mentored His disciples into, you are tormenting generations. The cry is, **"Help us produce mentors for the next generations."** The forerunners for the next generation need the mentoring of those who have gone before. The great mentors need to come out of retirement. You might not have the physical strength to hoop and holler in the pulpits, but in the privacy of your homes or in some other setting, you have the ability to impart life. There is always mentoring work to do. This generation is crying along with generations that have gone before them. We need mentors that can help silence the cries and dry the tears of those of this generation who are seeking someone to advise, teach, and coach them into successful, fruitful living. We are to transport the desperate cries of the anguish in our city streets into the Kingdom, transforming their cries of anguish into cries of joy, praise, and a desire to want more of Jesus Christ the Messiah.

As my life has begun to take the form and shape of the Kingdom of our Father, there has been a silencing of my own inner cries and memory of a tormented past—they are being erased with every stroke of his divine touch. I have counted my experiences for this generation's gain. For, if we don't mentor or advise, teach and coach after the Kingdom of the God, we are heading further in the direction of a king-doomed society and church. We must mentor and develop this generation after the way of righteousness

Chapter Two
The Torn-mentor

Through my observations, I notice that a great deal of the Christian community is torn. People who are torn are hardly good prospects for effective mentors. There is nothing worse than a torn advisor, teacher or coach, because they mentor from inside their pain, and not from outside of it. They will advise, teach, and coach you into bondage. When you are torn, you are in torment, which means to be in great pain or anguish. Torment is a source of pain. It causes great physical pain or mental anguish. Torment also means to annoy or harass. People who are torn in most cases become torn-mentors. When a mentor has not totally yielded himself in obedience to the precepts and principles of the Kingdom of God, they have not totally girded themselves, which makes them open door opportunities for demonic influences. If they are not healed from past experiences, it can affect their mentoring ability.

This generation does not seem to be able to overcome this principality that is attacking them, because the generation before them did not conqueror or defeat the principality that attacked them. These mentors now advise, teach and coach this generation, and whatever a generation does not defeat or conquer carries over into the next generation. Generational curses go far beyond our natural families; there are some spiritual curses that we inherit from our spiritual mentors and parents as well. Whether it is spiritual or natural, people are only capable of reproducing in their offspring what they are. In other words, if you have been mentored by someone torn, you were probably torn in the process. If the traits of your tormenting haven't surfaced yet, it's probably because you have not yet stepped into an area of leadership that would "reveal" them.

Most people will never know just how torn they are until they enter into marriage, parenting, or any other type of covenant relationship that includes advising, teaching, and coaching—mentoring! We never know what is truly inside of us until people begin to pull on us, and it all begins to unravel. Some people think they have escaped certain experiences without scars and wounds, until they are engaged in a relationship with another imperfect being. We are all a product of our experiences, and you can believe that there has been transference of that spirit. There was an affect that might not manifest in the same fashion, but there was an affect.

Whether you are consciously or unconsciously aware of the spirit that was transferred to you by your torn-mentor, he or she has gained an opportunity to advise, teach or coach—and what will be released is what has been imparted. Frustrations with your own torments could lead you to become very defensive about your own issues, or very easily offended, and a brother or sister offended is harder to win than a fortified city. You will probably, at some point, come across as harsh, dominating, and controlling to those you mentor. Position probably will mean everything to you now that you are in charge.

One of my flaws as a leader was that I would not trust my life or the ministry that God gave me to be governed by any organization, because of my personal experiences and also because I was a man that was always used to being in control. I had to dominate. Even as a pastor, I would delegate authority but not grant total control. It was hard for me to completely let go; that was a damaging flaw to the ministry. The spirit of competition was the driving force. You are also at risk for being driven by your own selfish ambitions, shielding and protecting yourself from becoming close to anyone— surely an unhealthy trait for a mentor whose exposure and availability are of the utmost importance. Transparency is the key to successful mentoring.

SHELTER FROM TORMENT

As a father, I am led to do what most parents do not do. That is— most parents spend too much time sheltering their children from outside influences, keeping them away from the things that will one day get a hold to them anyway. My job as a father is not to hide and shelter my children from this world. Because of my torn past, that would only cause mental, emotional, physical, and spiritual pain. It is in their best interest to train them to confront certain catastrophic experiences. Most people shelter and alienate their children because they are afraid that the same thing that happened to them will happen to their children. But what we don't realize is that being overly protective will eventually breed rebellion. I believe my mother was strict and sheltered my sisters because of her experiences as a child; but eventually my sisters became silent rebels when they reached a certain age. My job as a father is to prepare my children, so that when or if they encounter difficult experiences, they will know how to deal with and overcome them. As a father and mentor, my advice, teaching, and coaching starts at home. Many parents have the spirit of Eli: they think they are doing well at raising everyone else's children, while their own escape the benefits they claim others are gaining.

I think somehow we avoid our own families and put the focus on ministry family. In my opinion, neither one is any more important than the other—both require the same thing: the training of a child in the way of the Lord. Parents do well in preparing their children (natural or spiritual) for success in life, but they lack the ability to prepare them for the challenges that come with failure and the ability to get back up afterwards. This is because we have not dealt with our own failures, gotten over our own dilemmas, or gotten back up again. Oh yes, of course we moved on physically, but most people, believe it or not, are still haunted and tormented by their past. So many in the Body of Christ whose mega ministries have hidden or camouflaged their mega torment, or whose natural successes have covered up the real issue behind why they are going on a third marriage, or who have children who are not a part of their lives, or their unconquered lust runs rapid in their lives, lay torn.

Torment has produced fornicators and adulterers; and because they have not dealt with the rape and molestation that has been shut up in their hearts, we have leaders who are insecure and do not trust the other gender. In some cases, their sexuality has been thrown off and they have been conformed into bisexuals, lesbians, and homosexuals. They are in the forefront of ministry, tormenting those they should be mentoring—releasing feminine men, and women who seem to have more testosterone than men. These torn individuals have not dealt with their own hurts, pain, failures, and disappointments. This is why we have drill sergeants, bosses, correctional officers, principals, and leaders who are disproportionately strict as torn-mentors and leaders.

To be transparent is very relevant for mentors, because those we are mentoring learn from our mistakes. Until the forerunning generation overcome what has been tormenting them, generation after generation will produce more and more torn-mentors. This will be even worse than the prior because as scripture reminds us, with each generation it gets worse. A look at the communities and regions of our world reveals the decay from the influence of tormentors. If we look at the leaders in most of our churches, we see evidence of unconquered, unhealed torment. We have witnessed on television the failure of great men and women of God, and we never know why they did what they did, but we know something was left unconquered. Men don't molest boys simply because they have a desire to, there has to be some history somewhere. We don't wake up one morning and become what's just been exploited publicly, there had to be a personal struggle that was likely birthed out of our own experiences that went unaddressed earlier in our life. What's not detected and dealt with as a child will flourish when we become adults and relentlessly torment the lives of others, thus perpetuating the tormenting cycle.

PARTIAL TRUTHS, PARTIAL OBEDIENCE: REBELLION IN THE TORN-MENTOR

Let's now consider Saul, who suffered from what I call partial truth and partial obedience. Partial truth is when you tell half the story, but not the other half. Similarly, partial obedience is to intentionally half do what you were instructed to do. Both eventually invite rebellion to enter into your spirit. We have in 1 Samuel 10:14-16 an example of partial truth.

And Saul's uncle said unto him and to his servant, Whither went ye? And he said, To seek the asses: and when we saw that they were nowhere, we came to Samuel. And Saul's uncle said, Tell me, I pray thee, what Samuel said unto you. And Saul said unto his uncle, He told us plainly that the asses were found. But of the matter of the kingdom, whereof Samuel spake, he told him not Then, also, we have Saul's sinful offering. First Samuel 13:7b-9 says: *As for Saul, he was yet in Gilgal, and all the people followed him trembling. And he tarried seven days, according to the set time that Samuel had appointed: but Samuel came not to Gilgal; and the people were scattered from him. And Saul said, Bring hither a burnt offering to me, and peace offerings. And he offered the burnt offering.*

When Saul did this, he instituted himself into an office he did not qualify for. Verses 10-14 explain the consequences of disobeying God's spokesman, which results in the kingdom being seized from his hands. In 1 Samuel 14:19, you will see where Saul told a priest to withdraw his hand. In other words, do not consult God now, there is no time. Then there is an incident in 1 Samuel 14:24-30 that lets us know that Saul so desired to avenge himself against his enemies, that he neglected the needs of his own men and swore a foolish oath that almost cost the life of his son. This is an example of a torn-mentor in the making. Lastly, we have his partial disobedience in 1 Samuel 15:3, where word came from the Lord saying, *"Now go and smite Amalek, and utterly destroy all that they have, and spare them not; but slay both man and woman, infant and suck- ling, ox and sheep, camel and ass."* Verse 9 lets us know that despite the instructions given, *"...Saul and the people spared Agag, and the best of the sheep, and of the oxen, and of the fatlings, and the lambs, and all that was good, and would not utterly destroy them: but everything that was vile and refuse, that they destroyed utterly."* The rest of the chapter explains how the Lord rejected, refused, and took the kingdom from Saul.

Partial truth and partial obedience equals rebellion. Rebellion is armed resistance to one's government, and it is defiance of any authority. First Samuel 15:23a states, *"For rebellion is as the sin of witchcraft, and stubbornness is as iniquity and idolatry."* The Hebrew word for rebellion means bitterness or unpleasant. It's a masculine noun meaning obstinacy, or stubbornness. Use of the term consistently stays within this tight semantic range and most often describes the Israelites determined refusal to obey the precepts laid down by the Lord in his law. It is nearly impossible for someone to produce in others what has not been produced within themselves. You cannot give the Kingdom of God if you have not received it.

> TRAIT: "Rebellion and bitterness is the bloodline trait of the torn-mentor."

Whatever childhood, teenage, or young adult experience Saul had, had made him very rebellious and bitter inside. Whether it was a strict upbringing or some catastrophe, it caused him to be full of rebellion, bitterness, stubbornness, and disobedience. Torn-mentors are those who refuse to be governed by authority and submit only to their own. The torn-mentors of our day are rebels against Christ, holding religion as truth. The reason I say this is because religion has tormented and torn so many lives, and offended so many people.

CAUSES FOR REBELLION IN THE TORN-MENTOR

Now, if I can just shift for a moment in an effort to not only describe a problem, but to offer a solution, the first step is always to identify "the cause." I would like to talk about what produces rebellion, bitterness and resentment, as these are the roots or nourishment for torn-mentors. I believe that "unforgiveness" is why rebellion exists. Consider the meaning of rebellion: armed resistance to one's government. The most likely cause of most rebelliousness in a given area is that those that rebel have been hurt or torn in the area of authority they are resisting or rebelling against. Most people who cannot submit to their own pastor's authority could have been wounded by other pas- tors they were under; and even though their current leader shows no obvious sign of being a tormentor, they have been experientially conditioned to refuse to give anyone else another opportunity to hurt them because they have not forgiven and gotten over the experiences. Now this concept pertains to all areas. So many marriages are full of individuals who rebel against the word of God concerning their spouses because of constant hurt and torment in prior marriages or relationships. Never forgiving and getting over the previous experience they become bitter and resentful towards their cur- rent spouse. Unforgiveness will manifest itself in all your relation- ships, and some individuals can hold bitterness or unforgiveness for months, even years, tearing themselves apart and everyone they come in contact with.

Let's even consider that this is the reason why there are so many uncovered and independent churches in our cities: unforgiveness will turn a healing, loving sermon, into a good lashing or beat down message. I call it a subtle way of torment—the "pulpit torment"— taking your frustrations out on your congregations.

This is why a person who has not totally submitted to God's reign and authority rejects it.

The reign of Saul ends like this: *"But the Spirit of the Lord departed from Saul, and an evil spirit from the Lord troubled him"* (1 Samuel 16:14). The evil spirit was used as an instrument of judgment on Saul, resulting in a mental disturbance bordering on madness. Saul's servants suggested that they seek the skill of a cunning harp player to soothe Saul's mental torment.

Let me provide a footnote on this because a lot of people think that God sent an evil spirit upon Saul, but that is not true. The evil spirit is Saul's reaction as a result of God renting the kingdom from him. So David, the son of Jesse, Saul's successor, took the harp and played with his hand. Saul was refreshed and the evil spirit departed from him. This was only a temporary fix. This is the birth of a torn-mentor. Disobedience and rebellion will always lead to the fulfillment of Deuteronomy 28:28: *"The Lord shall smite thee with madness, and blindness, and astonishment of heart."* Because we are dealing with ministry, the type of torn-mentor Saul was becoming is most relevant to this chapter.

When you are still in a leadership position and know that God has rejected you, and the people are beginning to question and reject your leadership, you will torment those that seem to have the potential to take your place. Saul was in the process of seeing the God who rejected him accept David, someone whom he himself had mentored. Saul was about to witness someone he mentored succeed where he had failed, and even accomplish things that he did not.

> *And David went out whither so ever Saul sent him, and behaved himself wisely: and Saul set him over the men of war, and he was accepted in the sight of all the people, and also in the sight of Saul's servant. And it came to pass as they came, when David was returned from the slaughter of the Philistine, that the women came out of all the cities of Israel, singing and dancing to meet King Saul with tabrets, with joy, and with instruments of music. And the women answered one another as they played and said Saul hath slain his thousands, and David his ten thousands. And Saul was very wroth and the saying displeased him: and he said, they have ascribed unto David ten thousands, and to me they have ascribed but thousands: and what can he have more but the Kingdom?*
> —1 Samuel 18:5-9

This type of attitude can only come from someone who has not embraced the Kingdom of God. Mentors begin to torment when they feel that their "personal kingdom" is threatened. I speak this specifically to pastors, ministers, and leadership in general, because when a leader's position is threatened by someone who is being celebrated by the people, mainly the person they are mentoring, it invites an ugly spirit of jealously.

The relationship of Saul and David was fine: Saul just being in the presence of David's harp playing brought relief to his torment. Just knowing that he had someone to bring victory and celebration to his perceived kingdom, instead of strife and frustration, was a consolation. David, in his mind and heart, finally found the mentor or father he so longed for, seeing that his natural father and mentor never acknowledged he existed—he kept him sheltered by hiding him behind the scenes and holding him hostage from purpose. For David, the connection with Saul was the consummation of a dream come true. Saul was someone who pushed him and celebrated who he was. Saul gave David a mentoring platform: he advised, instructed, and coached him in putting his true anointing to use. He did not keep him where he thought he would fit, but he used him in the area of his anointing. For David, this is what he always wanted. Saul taught and coached him, even if it was but for a season. To David, it was the fulfillment of destiny. The Bible does not say in detail, but consider it through Saul's actions: he advised, taught, and coached David. He kept David in his presence, until the day the people celebrated David more than Saul. When that happened, the "mentor" became the "torn-mentor."

So many in this generation are torn because they are under mentors or leaders who cannot handle anyone else in the house being celebrated. Our job is to push those who are coming behind us to go further than where we are, advise them well; to deliberate and resolve issues and conflict. Good advice will always lead to promotion.

Teach them and coach them, so that they exceed your own failures. The people that you mentor are a product or a reflection of you, o should I say the Christ in you. I am reminded that I attended a church were the leader was very dominate and controlling; and as long as you did things his way you were correct. One particular Sunday morning we had a very high service and the spirit of the Lord moved on me and another minister. We began to lay hands on a teenager that was demonically bound, and while there was clear manifestation of the teens deliverance in motion, in the middle of the service he stopped us and said, "Don't. No one has that type of authority in the house but him." That was the beginning of my torment .

As I write about this, I recall so vividly how the house used to get excited when my pastor would have me preach. It got to the point where I became the sermon. It eventually progressed to no one else in the pulpit could be served water but him—those were his instructions he gave over the pulpit. So much began to go on, and things grew tormentingly worse that I eventually moved from the pulpit to the pews.

I no longer desired or needed to share the pulpit with a man who started out as my "mentor" but became my "tormentor." I thought I finally found the man that would make up all the years I spent searching for instruction and instead it felt as if Saul himself was resurrected from the dead "just for me." No matter where I went I was proud because I was representing him and the church. I tried hard to please him, but in torment I continuously failed. I even preached the way I preached—with power and anointing. I did what I did to get results because I wanted his approval, I wanted him to say good job, wonderful message, but I got the Saul eyes! It seemed even Saul's javelins had been excavated, and I found myself ducking and dodging them. There was first a resurrection of "Saul," and then of his "devices."

There should be no greater joy to a mentor than to see the person, the mentee, slaying and facing their own giants—conquering areas that were failures in their own generation and personal life. For those of you who are mentees in ministry, do not get annoyed or jealous when the spirit of God is moving and the service is stopped because Saul thinks he is the only one that has God's anointing; or when the Sauls of this world think they are the only ones in the house that has the authority or power to push the enemy back.

For those of you who are mentors in ministry, what a privilege and honor it should be for you to mentor the generation that is going to usher in the next move of God. The tormenting spirit is an attack from the enemy to try and stop the shift and repositioning of the army of God from standing again in the forefront. The torn-mentor in his rebellion and disobedience, is attacked with envy, jealousy, intimidation, and thoughts of failure. This causes him to become a vision-killer of those under his leadership. Let's have some food for thought: both Saul and David pursued each other. Saul pursued David because he wanted to kill him. David pursued Saul because he loved him and wanted his mentor's love and acceptance. In spite of how bad Saul wanted to destroy David's life, David desperately wanted this torn-mentor's love.

THE REJECTION OF A TORN-MENTOR

Now think for a moment: in his natural life, David was rejected, overlooked, confined, always pushed aside, and tormented by his biological father Jesse. He had a father that ignored him; and while everybody else was being groomed to possibly be considered the next king, David was silently and lovingly grooming and keeping sheep despite the rejection, neglect, and torment he felt in his heart. While all of his brothers were accepted by his father, he was rejected. Rejection is the worst kind of torment—there is nothing like loving someone and wanting their love in return, only to be met with rejection. Rejection can turn our hearts in another direction— far off course from where God wants us to be.

David then joined the kingdom and experienced twice as much torment than he did at home. There is no pain greater than the pain that comes from being hurt by someone you believed God put in your life to console and guide you. I mean, when your natural mother and father forsake you, your spiritual parents and mentors are your final hope. In a sense, this pain is greater because healing from the first experience has taken place; there was rest, restoration, and a release. So, to be healed from an experience only to be crushed by the same experience again is more devastating than the first.

After you have thought about what I said, consider the words from a man who was tormented. David said in Psalm 55:12-14

> *For it was not an enemy that reproached me; then I could have borne it: neither was it he that hated me that did magnify himself against me; then I would have hid myself from him. But it was thou, a man mine equal, my guide, and mine acquaintance. We took sweet counsel together, and walked unto the house of God in company.*

There is a word that stands out in this verse, and that word is guide. A guide is someone who leads or directs another in his ways. One who directs a person in his conduct or course of life; one who supervises or influences. There is a Hebrew word for guide which is **nachah** (naw-khaw), a primitive (basic or origin) root word which means to guide or lead; by implication to transport, bestow, bring, govern, and lead; to put or straiten. This is a verb meaning to lead usually in the right direction or on the proper path. In other words, a guide can very well be a mentor. David describes his traitor's actions in Psalm 55:20-21, which states:

> *He hath put forth his hands against such as be at peace with him: he hath broken his covenant. The words of his mouth were smoother than butter, but war was in his heart: his words were softer than oil, yet were they drawn swords.*

This was a mentor who became a tormentor. This text does not really say who the traitor is, but hear with the spirit, the words of

THE CRY OF A GENERATION:
The Torn-Mentor

David. He hath put forth his hands against such as to be at peace; for each attempt Saul made on his life, David made an attempt to be at peace with Saul. David said: "He hath broken his covenant."

The covenant of love that releases the power of care and concern was broken—the covenant in Ephesians 6:4 that states: *"And, ye fathers, provoke not your children to wrath: but bring them up in the nurture and admonition of the Lord."* The covenant that Paul also wrote in Colossians 3:21 which states, *"Fathers, provoke not your children to anger, lest they be discouraged,"* was also broken. The covenant in Deuteronomy 6 that God gave parents and mentors, so that they themselves could be in covenant with Him—so that their son and their son's sons or daughters could be taught covenant relationship through their parents and mentors was broken. This charge goes beyond the chronological child that needs instruction, but it also applies to that spiritual child that God needs to subdue the earth and exercise His providence.

Listen to the words of David, who says the words of his mouth were smoother than butter, but war was in his heart. Just think of all the words of encouragement that Saul spoke to David that caressed his spirit, mind and heart; words of inspiration, appreciation, and acceptance as David went out for him. These were the words that erased and healed him from his natural experiences; words that brought life and revival in David's life, and promoted his ministry until the day he was celebrated. Saul's words were deceitful and manipulative. David's success revealed the very thing that Saul the tormentor needed deliverance from.

Rebellion, disobedience, and war were already in his heart. Consider the words of Mark 7:18-22:

> ...Are ye so without understanding also? Do ye not perceive, that whatsoever thing from without entereth into the man, it cannot defile him. Because it entereth not into his heart, but into the belly, and goeth out into the draught, purging all meats? And he said, That which cometh out of the man, that defileth the man. For from within, out of the heart of men, proceed evil thoughts, adulteries, fornications, murders, thefts, covetness, wickedness, deceit, lasciviousness, an evil eye, blasphemy, pride, foolishness.

All these things come from within and defile the man. We already know from 1 Samuel 8:10-18 the manner of man Saul was. It was just camouflaged—hidden in his looks. So one can even go as far as to say that the chosen revealed the truth about the appointed. God sometimes intentionally (I believe) puts a torn-mentor in the lives of His people, those of which He calls, in order to:

1)   Propel them into an area of leadership.
2)   Make them aware not to put those they are leading and mentoring through the same thing.
3)   Prep them to deal with those they will encounter who have been tormented.
4)   Help them appreciate God Himself.

Let's look at David's last statement. He said his words were softer than oil, yet they were as drawn swords. Oil represents the anointing, and can be interpreted as his words carried with them a certain power that ministered to David at one point in time. But they were only words to draw him close enough to slay him. This individual that David is describing has to be Saul, a mentor who turned into a torn-mentor. Only a person who has the ability to minister to you in such a way can get you close enough to draw a sword that will pierce the heart. This is a subtle act from someone close. The torn- mentor has character and personality issues. The only healing source for the torn-mentor is to see God outside himself, and to deal with his personal issues and struggles honestly.

This means stepping inside the matrix and becoming a duplicate of Jesus Christ. Jesus is the matrix for the Kingdom of God here on earth. The matrix is that which is within—something else originates or develops from it. A matrix is an electro-phonogram where mass produced from the original is duplicated. There is a Hebrew word for matrix, which is <u>rechem</u> (rek-em), which means the womb. The womb is a fetus by which birthing takes place. Jesus Christ is the womb or fetus for the Kingdom of God; He is the matrix, "the reload," being birthed in the Kingdom through Christ. He heals the torn areas in a mentor's mind, heart, and spirit. Until the torn-mentor steps inside the matrix of the Kingdom of God, regeneration is impossible. Until regeneration by the Holy Spirit takes place, generation after generation will produce even more torn-mentors.

When a person is torn on the inside, it affects their ability to treat people the way that God has designed for us to treat each other. There are many leaders in our society and in our churches whose lives have been torn. There are hearts that have been torn and scarred beyond human repair. Torn-mentors are the most dangerous people on the planet. Rapists, serial killers, child molesters, gang bangers, homosexuals, lesbians, abusive men, and insecure women are all people who have been tormented in some form or fashion. I believe that what people act out on others communicates what they have experienced themselves.

A torn-mentor is an individual that needs repair—they are torn! We live in such a condemning and judgmental society that even when someone appears to be torn or act based upon past experiences that have torn them, we can be merciless and unforgiving, and tear them even more. A person that is torn knows they are, especially those of us who have invited Christ in our lives, because He brings to the surface and deals with those inner, hidden things that we have covered, concealed, and refused to deal with. The truth of the matter is a torn-mentor is someone who has been scarred or torn by a mentor. Think about the reason why you are the way you are, why you treat people they way you do, why you do to others what you do. As a matter of fact, think about the way you raise your children or how you act in relationships. Is it because you have a scar and have not completely healed?

# Chapter Three:
When the Torn-mentor Mentors:
The Law of Transference and Reproduction

Because mentoring is a deposit of life from one vessel into another, when the torn-mentor mentors, he reproduces himself in those he mentors. This is the law of transference, not only of spiritual life but also of natural. One writer says that you can have all the knowledge in the world, but you only produce in people what you are. No matter how hard we would like to or even try to make lives better in those we mentor, we can only give them what we have—nothing more, nothing less.

I believe that most people try to relive their lives through their children or those they mentor, and try to produce in them what they always wanted to become or achieve but never did. This in itself can cause torment because there is nothing more frustrating than trying to produce something in someone that you do not have or that you are lacking. And because mentoring is more of a transference of spiritual life, you can only deposit the amount of life or the kind of life you have.

If you have life you produce life; if you have little life you produce little; and if you have no life you produce no life at all. It is sad to say, but when you look at our world, both in the secular and spiritual (religious), it has produced nothing more than what has been the norm. It makes me think when I look at politics, church, and our world and see the same torments, flaws, and characteristics plaguing all three elements. It seems as though in all three areas, each generation is reproducing the generation before, but producing nothing better. This is a type of iniquity which has passed from generation to generation, and continues to spread like a virus because no one can stop. This is the Law of Reproduction.

When a mentor fails to take the proper time to heal from certain experiences, receive counsel or even experience a change from being in the presence of God, they will unconsciously put individuals through the same or similar experiences and reproduce themselves. We should consider the importance of producing a generation that can accomplish what we did not and succeed where we failed. Being a concerned father of four girls and one son, I am reminded constantly of the importance of not allowing them to live under the same fatherless, impoverished conditions that I lived in.

There's a certain mindset that comes with living in poverty and growing up without a father. Eventually, I realized the necessity to break that iniquity or that curse that my father passed to me. I began to give my own son growing up the semblance of life without a father—that is a torment in itself. I will tell you, even at one point my daughters could have suffered from emotional torment because of a home that ended up in divorce. They had to deal with the mere fact that they had two bitter, angry, resentful parents who lived in separate homes and were forced to start over again from scratch. Two parents who took all their frustrations out on their little innocent children, placed them in the line of fire, and robbed them of the comfort of loving, caring parents who really didn't understand the importance of getting over their problems for their children's sake. Our children were subject to unnecessary torment.

I mention this experience because if I had not caught myself, they could have very easily been potential victims of circumstance, and pushed in the direction of gangs, drugs, or prostitution—or turned out by a pimp who showed them a deceptive kind of love. They could have ended up in multiple relationships, looking for something that their father should have shown them; or even pregnant by some playboy who said I love you just to indulge in sexual activity—this is reproducing torn-mentors.

Most torn-mentors do not even realize that they are reproducing themselves because psychologically they have convinced themselves that they are healed, or even worse, don't realize they are damaged. This is even more common in the religious community (the church). The church is reproducing more torn-mentors than ever before. It is obvious because every time you turn on the television, some pastor or minister of the gospel is shamefully exposed and caught up in some scandal. For some, they are only reliving or acting out what they have been sheltering for years: a negative past experience, but in any case here they are, reproducing themselves in others. The quantity of torn-mentors in the church is the church's fault. We have lowered our standards and accepted statutes and decrees over holiness. Thus, this type of behavior is accepted when leaders camouflage their torment with certificates and present themselves as holy.

From the beginning, God had one intent only, and that was to tabernacle Himself inside of His people and create an offspring in His image and likeness, transferring Himself within His people. This is a biblical truth and fact: when God created Adam in His image and after His likeness, He intended His offspring to be born the same way—the possibility of torment was not even a prospect until Adam failed to keep God's charge (Genesis 1-3). Romans 5:12 states:

> *Wherefore, as by one man sin entered into the world, and death by sin; and so death passed upon all men, for that all have sinned."* Romans 5:19 states: *"For as by one man's disobedience many were made sinners, so by the obedience of one shall many be made righteous.*

I brought these two scriptures up as reference to show that transference is not a theory but a fact. Just as an individual can very well be damaged by an experience and forced into torment by the fault of another, that same person can willingly receive redemption and healing by fulfillment of another. Let the healing process begin! So, for the torn-mentor, he or she does not have to mentor torn. There does not have to be a transfer of death to those that are mentored by torn-mentors.

The most embarrassing thing for a mentor is for the person that they are mentoring to know that they have vulnerabilities, pain, or even tormenting experiences that they have not gotten over. Some mentors have leprosy (revealing of the flesh). Sometimes it's not the pain of our past that we are hiding; sometimes it can be the fleshy sins of our present that we are revealing that's tormenting lives.

It's interesting how some people can be ashamed and embarrassed about others finding out about certain events, but not a bit bothered by the person being affected by their abuse or torment. There has to come a point in a torn-mentor's life when he or she is tired of tormenting lives and reproducing him- or herself in others. Torn-mentors must become tired of transferring their torment into innocent lives, imparting anger, resentfulness, lust, and bitterness into the future's next leaders.

While we are on this line of talking, I am reminded of one of the most misunderstood, untaught scriptures ever: it is the prayer of Jabez found in 1 Chronicles 4:9 it is a prayer that is often used to express a petition for more prosperity, but I believe that this prayer was a desperate cry for more than that. I believe this for a few reasons: First, because his mother bore him in pain. Now just for thought, was it the pain of birth or the pain of torment while bearing him alone, fatherless? Second, his name mean*t pain*. Third, because in his prayer, *1 Chronicles 4:10, NKJ states: "And Jabez called on the God of Israel saying, 'Oh, that You would bless me indeed, and enlarge my territory, that Your hand would be with me, and that You would keep me from evil, that I may not cause pain!' So God granted him what he requested."*

I do not want to delve too deeply into this, but just challenge yourself for a moment to think outside of the religious box. Jabez asked the Lord to enlarge his territory. A territory is a piece of land within a land that does not have full capacity. I believe that Jabez's cry was to have full capacity of the Kingdom of God. Why? Because all his life he was exposed to pain. Just maybe he wanted the hand of the Lord to familiarize him with something other than pain. He also said, "Keep me from evil that I may not cause pain." This sounds like our culprit: a potential tormentor who was familiar with pain all his life. His mother bore him with pain, and she named him pain. She may have inflicted pain upon him because of her own pain. And, because of his pain, he afflicted pain on others until he reached the point in his life where he was tired of being afflicted with pain and afflicting others with pain. In his tiredness, he called out to God that the full capacity of His Kingdom would come upon him. Lord, make me a "mentor" and not a "torn-mentor!"

This was mentioned just to challenge your thinking; this prayer of Jabez needs to become the prayer of the torn-mentor. Until the torn-mentor begins to cry out for the Lord to expand his territory within his heart, put His hand upon him, and keep evil from him so that he can no longer cause pain and reproduced another torn-mentor, his or her heart cannot be healed from a tormented past. He will continue to reproduce what he is.

As mentioned in the previous chapter, Saul was a torn-mentor who tore David's life. David, in return, became worse than his torn-mentor through his actions with Uriah, and even reproduced in his offspring what he was—ten times worse. He produced a son who raped and took his own sister's virginity; sons who were full of lust and who loved many strange women; sons who slaughtered their own brothers and rebelled against David himself, causing him to flee. When torn-mentors mentor, the generation that they are mentoring are twice as worse as the previous. In order for our world and church to produce well and capable leaders, every leader or mentor has to take some kind of accountability and be responsible for how they advise, teach and coach others. They must stop using their torment as an inner excuse to justify why they are doing what they are doing.

I could discuss experiences during my upbringing that I have been silent about for years, such as being sexually molested by women in my family, and they called it training. I could talk about gang life, drugs, the years I spent in prison, or the years I spent outside of prison feeling abandoned, forsaken, and alone. Being afflicted with pain all my life could have very well reproduced a torn-mentor, but instead the Lord used my affliction and experiences to help heal the torn in the body of Christ.

At one point I found it hard to believe that God could use someone who was as torn and wrecked as I was to heal lives. Deacons, ministers, pastors, and others would secretly seek after my counsel and come to my home and church for restoration. It even got to the point that the Lord was doing such a great work, that I believe Satan became extremely angry and started to attack my personal life, marriage, family, health and finances until eventually I lost all of it. I found myself alone, needing the very thing that I was giving out and no one seemed to be there for me. This started to produce bitterness, resentment, and anger; but at the same time it produced an understanding of what I was called to do and be to the Kingdom. No matter how hard I preached, I could not produce because I was doing so from inside my pain.

So, rather than reproduce what I was becoming, I had to relinquish my leadership role until I experienced complete healing and restoration by being in the presence of God. There was really no one to depend on, and even in that experience I still felt like the church was tormenting me because for some reason no one seemed to want to be near me. It was as if I had a contagious disease or something, and I could not figure out what was going on. Eventually, I realized that the enemy was using the very core of my ministry to assassinate the anointing of God on my life. Instead of wanting to produce mentors, I felt like tormenting those I thought or knew were tormenting me.

There was only one end and conclusion to that story. Through 1 Chronicles 4:9-10, I received the revelation and quickly began to proclaim my liberty in Christ and ask God to give me the full capacity of the Kingdom. In other words, I asked God to enlarge my territory. It is very easy to want to afflict pain on those whom you think are causing pain in your life. There are two types of torn-mentors, the intentional and the unintentional torn-mentor. The intentional torn-mentor is conscious of what he or she is doing and producing. They have a mindset that says since I was hurt, everyone else must hurt. They intentionally wound lives. The unintentional torn-mentor does not even realize that they are tormenting lives, their wounds are unintentional. They have no clue of the damage they have caused until it surfaces or someone else makes them aware of it. Some torn-mentors will even deny the fact that something is wrong with them and will make every attempt to say that the wounds are self-inflicted. A person who is not ready to take ownership is not ready for healing; they are still marinating in shame and guilt. So many torn-mentors are hiding behind their degrees or positions, which they see as more important than "lives."

ESCAPING THE TORMENTING

As children of God, the mandate from the beginning of creation has not changed, we are still called to be fruitful, multiply, replenish the earth, subdue it, and have dominion over it. We are to be converters in every sphere of our lives; but conversion starts with you so that replenishment is possible. To prevent your history from reproducing itself in someone else's life, you must allow the Kingdom of God to produce itself in your life. It is the life of Jesus

Christ that is supposed to flourish in our lives and the lives of those we mentor, not our experiences.

The very thing that was stripped from Adam is the very thing that we were born without, the image and likeness of God. For the torn-mentor, cloning prevention starts with reclaiming the image and likeness of God. I am really trying to avoid inundating you with a lot of scripture; however, it is nearly impossible because after all the writing and talking we do if in the end it doesn't direct you back to the Word of God, then complete healing and restoration is impossible.

When Adam was stripped of the image and likeness of God, it empowered the enemy to wreak havoc on God's creation. When humanity was stripped of their godly identity, it invited torment to wreck and shatter lives, and all creation. If you notice, soon after disobedience surfaced in the first family, jealousy, rejection, and anger, which lead to murder, tormented them—and this torment reproduced itself in every subsequent generation. After that, incest, curses, rape, murder, homosexuality, betrayal, slavery, adultery, war, etc., plagued the earth, continuously reproducing itself in mankind. Torn-mentors overpopulated the earth and now dominate the twenty-first century church, tearing lives apart. It is time to reclaim the image and likeness of God. For every torn-mentor that reclaims their identity in Christ, there are at least one to five individuals being mentored into purpose and destiny, and a torn-mentor being made whole.

I am often asked what is the image and likeness of God, and how does one achieve it? To simplify my explanation, I usually refer back to the beginning in Genesis 1:26, when God said, *"...Let us make man in our image and after our likeness."* In other words, God said let's reproduce ourselves in mankind. I believe God's statement was more concerned with spiritual attributes than physical appearance. Because God is a holy God, all His attributes are holy and blameless. Being made this way made it possible for Adam to keep God's charge to be fruitful, multiply, replenish, subdue, and have dominion over the earth. I believe God also expected Adam's offspring to be born exactly the same way He created Adam, in the image and likeness of God. When Adam yielded to disobedience and obeyed the voice of deception, he was immediately conformed to that which he yielded to, and that is why Romans 5:12 says: *"Wherefore, as by one man sin entered into the world, and death by sin; and so death passed upon all men, for that all have sinned."* Adam's disobedience released all types of torment into humanity, which caused his offspring to be born with flawed character, attitude and personality.

From Genesis to Malachi we see the activity of torn-mentor after torn-mentor. It was not until Matthew 5:3-14 that the image and likeness of God was taught and given back to humanity under the ministry of Jesus Christ. Jesus understood the importance of the image and likeness of God being restored to mankind before He could even begin to teach us how to live what God expected us to live. So in Matthew 5:1-14, we have what are called Beatitudes and Similitudes. The Beatitudes are a complete representation of what God is, or God's image. God is poor in spirit; He is always mourning to see change. He is meek and righteousness. He is merciful; He is a peacemaker and His heart is ever so pure. In His person in Christ, He was persecuted for righteousness sake: this is the image of God.

Until a torn-mentor recognizes the need to become poor in his spirit; lay aside wealthy pride and begin to mourn for change; stop acting like he or she is not affected by their past torment; become meek and endure their trials and tribulations without anger and resentment; hunger and thirst for a right standing with God; possess quality of character; and become a merciful peacemaker with a pure heart, he will continue to marinate in the torments of his past, and torment other lives.

In Matthew 5:13-14, Jesus said we are the salt of the earth, *"but if the salt have lost his savour, wherewith shall it be salted? It is thenceforth good for nothing."* You are also the light of the world. This is God's likeness or similarities: He is the salt of creation, but we are the salt of the earth, and salt is a preservative. Salt heals wounds, melts the coldness of men's hearts, seasons lives, and makes men thirsty for Him. This is what every torn-mentor must become, because this is what must be reproduced in the lives of those they mentor. We are the preservers of the earth, preservers of the next generation, healers of the earth, and healers of the next generation. We are called to melt the coldness of men's hearts and season the earth with the grace of the gospel—making this and the next generation thirsty for the Kingdom.

It is impossible for us to practice and live out the rest of the Sermon on the Mount without having the image and likeness of God restored to us. This is the only hope for the torn-mentor. Through the image and likeness of God, redemption and complete healing is available, preventing the emergence of more torn-mentors or people whose lives have been torn by those whom they thought had their best interests at heart.

THE URGENCY FOR A HEALED MENTOR

It's very disturbing when those who are called the salt of the earth have lost their savor, are unable to better lives, and have become the very reason why more lives are shattered and torn. What must happen is that the torn must reach the place of seeing the importance of a healed generation. The urgency for healed mentors is so critical for the healing of our world, church, and society. There can be no more reproducing of torn-mentors, we cannot allow another generation of torn-mentors to flourish. Our future mentors and leaders are now up-and-coming, and from my observations, even our teenagers and young adults are moving rapidly into the areas of leadership. Just by observing some of the things that they are struggling with and have not overcome, I can predict what mentoring and leadership is going to look like for the next twenty to fifty years. I have children that are coming behind those that are moving to the forefront, and watching them I can project what my sons and daughters will struggle with. We will produce another generation of torn-mentors unless those mentors who are hiding because of their experiences care enough to seek healing, come out of hiding, help lay firm foundations for the many to come, repair the breaches, and make our city streets safe again.

If I did not know God for myself, I would question His ability to transform lives. But I have gotten too familiar with Him and know for myself that with God nothing is impossible to those that believe. Our lives and walk with God must be filled with faith; and so instead of having faith in God and believing Him for houses, cars, money, spouses and mega ministries and churches, we need to believe God first that we can live the type of life that He taught in the Sermon on the Mount. We should also bear the fruit of the spirit that comes with it; the character, attitude, and personality. This will heal the mentor from being torn and prevent him or her from reproducing themselves in others.

When Christ downloads or deposits His life into our lives, it is He that works through us and allows us to do those things necessary to overcome what appears impossible to overcome. The plan of the enemy is to keep reproducing lives that are so full of torment, in order to halt the plans of God. Our generations that are moving forward to take our places, sadly, are lost. How horrific is their end—you are the hope! Yes you, the individual that is reading this book. Transformation for our future mentors starts with transformation of you. What you allow to build and make you, you will download into the lives of others. The questions I would like to ask is, what is your motive for ministry? How important is God to you? Is He so important that you are willing to be a sell-out?

How important is the generation coming behind you? These are just questions for thought because until a person really considers these questions and resolves them completely, the only important factor to them is "me and my house."

Sometimes, God would somehow allow me to stand outside myself and hear myself—it was in those moments that I realized I was torn. As long as you are isolated and not interacting with people you're fine; but people have a way of exposing the truth to you about you, even when they are not trying to. Even those in leadership roles can tell who you really are from those who are under your leadership; and for parents who think they are hiding, your children tell us who you are. It is God's principle that you transfer who and what you are into the lives of those you influence. Even though you are salt that lost its savor or, let me say, salt that's lost its saltiness, your life can be seasoned again.

You are, as I stated before, the preserver of the earth, the healer of the earth. It is through you that cold hearts will melt, lives will be seasoned by grace, and men and women will become thirsty for the Kingdom of God. Every individual that you come in contact with should leave your presence seasoned, thirsty, healed and preserved, but you yourself must be the same upon their encounter with you. The bottom line is that everyone that comes in contact with you, child of God, is going to receive a transference of something—the question is of what? Are you reproducing in them what you've been through, causing them to experience the pain and torment that you have experienced? Or, are you producing by example the life and character of Jesus Christ in them? If you are a concerned citizen of the Kingdom, then the latter should be your answer. I have observed the church closely and in my years of being saved and being in ministry, I have been involved in so many different functions and ministered the gospel in many churches. The amount of torn pastors, missionaries, ministers, choir members, and musicians that I have encountered was startling. I would ask myself how they can continue to function and operate in this condition, until I realized that a man or woman's pride will blind them from the truth. When we begin to take our life in Christ as serious as He does, then the lives of others will become as important as our own, and often times even more important than our very own.

Chapter Four
Refusing to Carry It Over

I believe that forgiveness is a starting point; it marks the beginning of a new life that says it stops here. There has to be a voice that cries out in this wilderness, that says I refuse to carry it over, I refuse to see another generation suffer because of someone else's lack of concern for the Kingdom's future. I want to see a shift. The preaching of John the Baptist marks an important shift in Kingdom history with a message that was repentance-centered. As a forerunner for a generation, he laid a foundation that would prepare his generation for the Lord's first coming. He preached repentance. Repentance is a change of mind that bears fruit in a changed life. The Hebrew meaning of the word means to think differently or afterwards, to reconsider, denoting change of place or condition; it also implies the feeling of regret or sorrow.

When we consider some of the torment we experienced, the hurt and pain that came from those who mentored, led or parented us, we have to draw some conclusion and say to ourselves, "I refuse to carry this over." When you reach the place of forgiveness through genuine repentance, you will refuse to carry your torment over into another generation of mentors and leaders. You very well know that damaged people are not equipped to mentor the Kingdom's future leaders. Even if you are thinking about becoming a mentor or just stepping into a major area of leadership, there has to be a time of healing in between the shift in your life—a period, as I stated in the former chapter, of rest and restoration, before release.

Refusing to carry it over simply means that you refuse to afflict others with your affliction or even refuse to wrestle and struggle with what your mentor wrestled and struggled with. You refuse to impart into your Kingdom relationships, or any other relationship, the same torment that you have experienced. Most of us have been tormented by church folks. Church hurt is the worst hurt to recover from because it can be so hard to forgive and forget what for many is their final hope. It is difficult for most people to recover and bounce back from church hurt, but your recovery is vital because "you" are the bridge that connects two generations. As Isaiah 58:12b states,

> *"Thou shalt raise up the foundations of many generations; and thou shalt be called, The repairer of the breach, The restorer of paths to dwell in."*

John the Baptist was a bridge builder, connecting two generations to the Kingdom of God by refusing to carry over the traditions and rituals that tormented so many in his time. He flourished at a time when shepherds were feeding themselves and not the flocks; when the diseased were not strengthened, the sick were not healed, the broken were not bound up; when those who were driven away were not sought after, and when they that ruled, ruled with force and cruelty. This dominated the religious community of John's day.

Having no mentor, John the Baptist was mentored and fathered by God. I want you to take note here: just as John the Baptist, the forerunner for Christ's first coming, was mentored and fathered by the Holy Spirit, so we, the forerunners of the Lord's final appearance, are and will be a product of the Father's personal encounter and outpouring, along with His word. When we understand the importance of this mandate, we will refuse to carry our negative experiences over. John refused to carry over what he was exposed to, but brought over what he was invoked by. He earned the nickname forerunner because he was the interlude for Christ's first appearance. Let us consider the price a forerunner pays.

As a forerunner, you experience and go through certain things to empower and enlighten you. The ultimate price you pay is death, and we are not talking about a physical death, but a spiritual one—dying to your emotional pain and desires. What this generation needs to see is mentors and leaders dying to self. Jesus, on a greater level even than John the Baptist, refused to carry His torment over, but died to it.

Consider our Lord and Savior's wilderness experience—every child of God must have one. The wilderness part of ministry is strictly training for endurance in tribulation. The wilderness is a time of trying and proving, to see who and what you put your trust in. Believe it or not, many of our mentors are still in the wilderness. They are mentoring, but they are doing it inside of their wilderness and bringing you inside their pain and torment by advising, teaching, and coaching you with a wilderness-mentality. A forerunner's experiences are for the consolation of those they mentor. The wilderness is the place where death becomes you, but also a place where life revives you. Before Jesus died physically on the two planks that some call a cross, He died to self in the wilderness. So, by the time He got to Calvary He was already dead. That is why he said in John 14:30: *"Hereafter I will not talk much with you: for the prince of this world cometh, and hath nothing in me."* Everything that could have possibly been used as a tool by the enemy against Christ to run interference on His ability to complete His cross, died off of Him in the wilderness. So at this point Satan had nothing in Jesus he could use to turn Him away from consummating the death and resurrection.

If you would briefly look at Matthew 4:4-11, I want to tell you why it is so important for you to die to your experiences. It is imperative that you do not carry them over and spill them into the next generation. The enemy's only aim was to prevent the power of the resurrection from being brought over. Without the power of the resurrection there can be no reclaiming the original image and likeness of God. Without the shedding of blood there is no remission of sins; therefore, if the cross was prevented there would have been no chance of regeneration or reconciling the kingdoms of the world back to God. The enemy only had two attempts:

before the cross and during the cross.

The attack in the wilderness was an assault against the character and personality of Jesus Christ. The outcome here would have determined what was carried over—thank God for Jesus Christ! The key here is to help identify what we must prevent from being carried over, which is the lust of the flesh, the lust of the eyes and the pride of life. Genesis 3:6a states:

> *And when the woman saw that the tree was good for food, and that it was pleasant to the eyes, and a tree to be desired to make one wise, she took of the fruit thereof."* 1 John 2:16 states: *"For all that is in the world, the lust of the flesh, and the lust of the eyes, and the pride of life, is not of the Father, but is of the world.*

This is what has been spilled over in every generation since Adam's fall, but the ability to conquer and overthrow it lies in Christ Jesus. Flawed character and corrupt personality that is a result of torn-mentors mentoring in the wilderness through failure, must proceed no further.

THE SPIRIT OF "INDEPENDENCE": A RESULT OF TORMENTING

The first thing we have to do is refuse to carry over the spirit of independence. This spirit says I don't need anyone, and in most cases it is the result of having been let down or tormented by people, which results in isolation. People who are independent are withdrawn from others and feel as though they can make it on their own, they do not trust others. Our dependence should be completely on God, not on ourselves or other people. Matthew 4:3-4 says, *"And when the tempter came to Him (Jesus), he said, If thou be the Son of God, command that these stones be made bread. But He answered and said, It is written, Man shall not live by bread alone, but by every word that proceeds out of the mouth of God."* If Jesus had yielded to the temptation of taking what God gave Him and using it for self-gratification, He would have spilled over in us the idea that it was okay to be independent and selfish.

Too many mentors are too dependent upon themselves, imparting that spirit in everyone that sits under their leadership. When you are too independent, no one can tell you anything because you know everything—at least most people who are independent think they do.

SHIFTING THE FOCUS OFF OF "US"

You have the resources to make it happen, you have ability, but building is far beyond having currency and resources. This generation does not need to see a bunch of rich, stuck-up, heady, high minded, mentors who are lovers of pleasures more than lovers of God. What needs to spill over are mentors full of Christ-like integrity. Jesus had the ability to turn the stones into bread and satisfy His earthly hunger, but He knew that there was a greater hunger that had to be satisfied more than just that of His own fleshly longings. He thought about everyone else except Himself those He came to reconcile back to the Father. He was so careful about what He carried over. When you walk with integrity, when the enemy makes an attempt to assassinate your character, you do not have to prove who you are or your capabilities, just continue to live what you are in Him. Mentors who have been torn are always trying to prove who they are to others and that they are so much more than what they appear to be.

The greatest in the Kingdom are those who serve and know how to serve correctly. Independence says I am not subject to the authority of others, I am self-sufficient, self-governed, and not affiliated with anyone. I am not requiring or relying on anyone else. I am not contingent, and I am not looking to others for opinions or for guidance in conduct. This is a rejection of mentoring, thus disqualifying you to "mentor." This is a self-destructive mentality that leads to failure in the mentor and mentee. This is why there are so many small, independent churches in our communities. The spirit of self-provision has been handed down from one generation to another; it is strong and dominates among believers. To tell you the truth, it is so dominate that it had spilled over into even Christian marriage. Christian marriages have become one big brawl because two individuals who refuse to submit to each other are always throwing their individualism in each other faces, which breaks the harmony and unity of the home structure wherein all relationships are interdependent.

One reason, I believe, that Jesus refused to carry over independency is because He knew that if He allowed Himself to get in the way of God's plan of salvation for all humanity, that it would have prevented the world from being reconciled back to God. Now as long as you allow yourself to get in the way of God's plan for you receiving complete healing and restoration, the people that you are called to lead to Christ will never get to Him, nor the power of His resurrection and the fellowship of His suffering. (Ok, so you're not really in a rush to get to that part, I understand.) Jesus died to it in the wilderness area of His ministry, which is another reason why we all must experience a wilderness. It is a place of dying to self and losing trust in your own ability, and living unto God and trusting Him by allowing His ability to work through you. I believe it is torment to lay a foundation of self-sufficiency by depending on resources, because man does not live by bread alone, but by every word that proceeds out of the mouth of God. The mentor needs to be mentored, and we all need each other.

THE DISILLUSIONMENT OF INVINCIBILITY

The second thing we have to be careful that we do not carry over is challenging your flesh: the mindset that says just because you are walking and living in Christ that you are beyond self-destruction, putting yourself in harm's way or going into areas that you know will tempt the God in you. In 1 Corinthians 10:9, the apostle Paul says *neither let us tempt Christ as some of them also tempted, and were destroyed of serpents.* Then he says in the twelfth and thirteenth verses: *Wherefore let him that think he stand take heed lest he fall. There hath no temptation taken you but such as is common to man: but God is faithful, who will not suffer you to be tempted above that ye are able; but will with the temptation also make a way to escape, that ye may be able to bear it.*

One of the greatest tricks of the enemy is to make men think that they are invulnerable. The greatest wakeup call to a person's life is when they thought it was impossible. So many mentors have at the hands of this spirit, found themselves in sin or falling into sin with those they mentor of the opposite gender, Oh! Nowadays even with gender of the same kind, they have become susceptible because of a false sense of invulnerability.

I have a number one rule that I apply to my own life: "Do not tempt God!" I will not put myself in situations anymore with people, places or things that I know will challenge my weaknesses. Even though I overcame almost all my weaknesses and they are areas of strength now, I will not play with fire. True Christians know their weaknesses and are aware of potential failure. Too many mentors have fallen because they live as though the struggle is over and it's not, it is only camouflaged. Testing yourself or thinking you stand is a game of Russian roulette and is setting you up for failure. When living for so many years independent of God, we are already at a disadvantage because we already come into it with challenges. We have enough temptations without having to prove what we can withstand, and there is no need to play daredevil.

The Christian life should be lived with confidence and caution, because the enemy is methodical, and we are not ignorant of his devices, but having him on our heel is close enough. Once again, Jesus knew who He was just as well as He knew what the consequences would be had He jumped from that pinnacle—He would have splattered. To be tempted only means to be tried, tested or proved; and when affiliated with God it is always intended for promotion. When Satan tempts you it is always intended for your failure and demotion. When you tempt yourself, it is self-destructive and suicidal.

The point I am getting at here is most mentors are too proud to admit that there are areas of weakness in their lives, and some of their actions were acts of foolishness through their own temptations. The generations that we are preparing who are coming behind us need to know and understand that they are not invincible or invulnerable, and that they should not linger in areas that can potentially jeopardize who they are.

I believe the desire to test and prove yourself is influenced by a combination of yourself and the enemy. Since Satan could not get Jesus to give in to independency and self-glorification, he tried to get Him to test His spiritual ability with acts of foolish carnality. In other words, he said I double dare you by saying in Matthew 4:6-7,

> *And saith unto Him, If thou be the Son of God, cast thyself down: for it is written, He shall give His angels charge concerning thee: and in their hands they shall bear thee up, lest at any time thou dash thy foot against a stone.*

Jesus said unto him, It is written again, Thou shalt not tempt the Lord thy God.

This is where pride usually slips in; pride always comes before destruction. Arrogance is a feeling or impression of superiority manifested in an unbarring manner of presumptuous claims. It also means exaggerating or disposed to exaggerate one's worth. Now pride is arrogance because pride is defined as an unduly high opinion of oneself; haughtiness, arrogance, dignity and self-respect; satisfaction in something done. Arrogance and pride are things that we cannot afford to carry over and spill in another generation.

This is the pride of life. The pride of life says, *"I will ascend into heaven, I will exalt my throne above the stars of God: I will sit also upon the mount of the congregation, in the sides of the north: I will ascend above the heights of the clouds; I will be like the most High"* (Isaiah 14:13a-14). This is the same pride that brought about Lucifer's fall that he planted in humanity in the Garden of Eden. Even though Adam and Eve where found lingering in tempting areas, hanging around the trees would not have killed them. How many times have we hung around something long enough until we eventually tampered with it? Because they were lingering around it lets me know they were already questioning whether or not they would die if they ate it. Am I "really" this vulnerable, or am I as "invincible" as the serpent suggests I am? Being in this state of mind and in question about what God said led the enemy to confirm what they already wondered in Genesis

3:4b,5: *"Ye shall not surely die: For God doth know that in the day ye eat thereof, then your eyes shall be opened, and ye shall be as gods, knowing good and evil."*

He planted the seed of being like God in their minds. The ultimate goal in carnal Christian's minds is to be like God; to proudly show our ability, not God's; and to impress those that marvel at our achievements. This type of mindset, too, stems from being tormented. A person who has not fully recovered can develop a spirit of self-dependency, which becomes the branch full of leaves of pride and arrogance.

Do not let pride and arrogance continue to destroy God's work. I refuse to spill pride or any other character defects or spiritual bondage in my children, or anyone I mentor. Consider what the wise King Solomon said in Proverbs 8:13: *"The fear of the Lord is to hate evil: pride, and arrogance and the evil way, and the froward mouth, do I hate."*

> In Proverbs 6:16-17 it states: *These six things doth the Lord hate: yea, seven are an abomination unto him: A proud look, a lying tongue, and hands that shed innocent blood. An heart that devise wicked imaginations, feet that be swift in running to mischief. A false witness that speak lies, and he that sows discord among brethren.*

Pride stands at the top. The reason pride is number one, I believe is because pride produces a lying spirit, and a lying spirit will lead a person to shed innocent blood to protect themselves or their circumstances. When a person sheds innocent blood; it is time to cover it up with wicked imaginations. You then run into all types of mischief, lying to sow discord among brethren. The feeling of spiritual invincibility means one first lies to "themselves." The Lord hates pride because it is the producer of every other type of evil. If I remember correctly, pride produced the five "I wills" in Lucifer and caused him to sow discord in God's Kingdom, start a revolt against God, and sow discord among the brethren in the heavens, which ended in him being expelled from Heaven (Isaiah 14:12).

Pride was the beginning of King David's falling into sin. It prevented him from going to war in the springtime when kings war, which led him to sin. We have to blame David's failure on pride because pride prevented him from being on the battlefield. Then he lied, shed innocent blood, his heart devised wicked imaginations, and on and on and on (1 Samuel 11:1).

So when the Lord sees pride, I believe He sees the very thing that turned His creation against His will, or that turned the closest person to Him into His one and only enemy. So move as far away from pride as possible Proverbs 16:18 states, *"Pride goeth before destruction, and an haughty spirit before a fall."* The wise king is only saying that pride is always in the forefront or leads in front of destruction, so whenever you see a proud spirit move out of the way so you will not get crushed by that tree, because it is coming down.

OVERCOMING THE SPIRIT OF PRIDE AND INVINCIBILITY

Mentors, overcome the spirit of pride with humility; do not carry the spirit of pride over forerunner; and produce fruit of the Father's Kingdom in those you are mentoring. The last of the three expresses the desire to achieve and fulfill the plan of God without price. I always say if you got something good and it seems to be of great value and you got it for nothing, it is probably too good to be true. I believe the easier it is for you to get something or even achieve something, the easier it is for you to let it go or lose it.

I know from experience that the things in my life that are most important to me are things that I had to suffer and fight for; things I worked hard for, such as the ministry of Christ in me, and my ability to write this book. It's not based on research but on experience. I lived out every phase of this manuscript, and the Holy Spirit put it together in written format. This is a generation that wants everything but is not willing to overcome or pay anything for it. They want it without price or at the expense of others; they are not willing to sacrifice their own time, effort, or lives for anything but will compromise their way through everything.

The gratitude and appreciation for something does not come without a good fight. The anointing of the Holy Spirit does not even come without a price. The last thing Jesus refused to carry over, which we all must refuse to as well, is compromise. The dictionary explains compromise as a settlement in which each side makes concessions; to adjust by compromise or to weaken. Compromise says, "Okay instead of going through all of that for this, I will give it to you for this." Hear the infamous plot of Satan to weaken the Christ as he makes one last attempt to get him to forfeit God's plan. He says in Matthew 4:8-10:

Again, the devil taketh Him up into an exceeding high mountain, and sheweth Him all the kingdoms of the world, and the glory of them. And saith unto Him, All these things will I give thee, if thou wilt fall down and worship me. Then saith Jesus unto him, Get thee hence, satan: for it is written, Thou shalt worship the Lord thy God, and Him only shalt thou serve.

This here is the point when most mentors give in. As I stated before, satan only had one goal and that was to prevent the cross. He wanted to prevent Jesus from carrying over the power of the resurrection —he wanted our Lord to end in failure like the first Adam, spilling over works of flesh. And, what better way to tempt the flesh after every other attempt failed. Let me sort of paraphrase what satan said to Jesus. He says I have the world in my hands. I subdued the earth from Adam and now exercise dominion over it. You came to reconcile this world back to God and bring it back under His reign and authority by suffering and dying to achieve your tasks. I make you an offer Jesus, for what you came to die for I will give it to you without price. No persecution, no piercing through the side, no mocking, no whipping with a whip laced with metal that every time it hits your flesh it rips it open at least a half inch deep. No nailing on a tree. I will give it to you without pain and suffering. You will experience no hurt if you would just worship me.

This also was a second chance for Satan to establish his kingdom above God's throne. If he could have convinced the final hope to yield to compromise, he would have achieved what he tried to achieve in Heaven. Man's desire for position, power, and prestige has always led him to compromise. Men will even compromise the move of God in their congregations to satisfy the desires of the flesh, or even just to build lives and churches that look good on the outside but are torn inside. Compromise is something that we really must refuse to carry over into the next generation, because the structure of the Kingdom will be as it always has been in times past: people with powerless positions. Jesus' mandate was to reconcile the regions of the world back to God by dying to the very thing that moved us from God: the desires of the flesh.

One other way to accomplish this was to let His righteousness exceed the righteousness of the scribes and the Pharisees, and to seize the Kingdom back from the enemy. satan knew Jesus was seeking to retrieve the Kingdom back one way or the other, so he figured he might tempt Him with compromise. If He had yielded to compromise (and his "foolish" attempt), satan would have still exercised dominion over the earth, unless God came up with another plan. But what other plan would there have been left after achieving a victory over the flesh in the first Adam and then turning around and achieving a spiritual victory over the second or the last Adam—Christ.

His submission to satan would have left him in charge and given him an eternal victory. Here is a golden nugget reader: whatever authority you submit to will be the authority that governs your life. Too many mentors have been governed by everything but the Kingdom of God—compromising who they are and what they stand for by failing to maintain their integrity.

I'll name a few things that people compromise for: men pleasing, tithes and offerings, membership, organization, infidelity, fame, and fortune. Everyone wants to build big reputations and seek glory for themselves. These forces must be defeated and pushed back. There are so many things that can be pleasing to our eyes, that can make one compromise, and that can blind the mentor or even those being mentored from the truth. When dealing with people that have been tormented, an easier way out is always appealing. A quicker or faster way always seems like the answer to momentary problems. People will do almost anything to stop the pain and suffering.

THE FOCUS FACTOR

The most important thing I believe you should remember is the focus factor. The focus factor is to stop looking at things through your own perception, and view them from a Kingdom perspective, because everything you go through is for a greater purpose. Now, your life is the point of contact: you experience success, struggles and suffering for someone else to connect with Christ. Take your focus off yourself and realize that your pain and suffering is for someone else's gain. Here is one of my favorite texts, Hebrews 12:1-2. *Wherefore seeing we also are compassed about with so great a cloud of witnesses, let us lay aside every weight, and the sin which doth so easily beset us, and let us run with patience the race that is set before us, Looking unto Jesus (the focus factor) the author and finisher of our faith; who for the joy that was set before him endured the cross, despising the shame, and is set down at the right hand of the throne of God*

Mentor, healed mentor, former torn-mentor or even the mentored- if that text in itself is not enough to make you leap for joy, it speaks for itself. It is self-explanatory. It keeps your eyes off everything except Christ. As I stated in a former chapter, just like your life is the before for someone else, He is the before for you. If He did it without compromise, so can "you!"

Compromise to the ears of those who have a false sense of direction sounds good, because it sounds better than pain and suffering. The truth that needs to be told about mentoring is that when your life has been designed to bring other people to a place of rest, restoration, and release, preparation will be lonely, frustrating, painful, burdensome, and with much tribulation and suffering; and you must do it without compromise. Some of the best potential mentors, and even the greatest of mentors, will never be, or are no more, because of compromise.

Here's another golden nugget: You have to go through your pain and suffering trusting God, in confidence and complete obedience. You must conquer pride and independency, because when tempted with compromise you are probably at a point where you are feeling lonely, forsaken, and abandoned. As a matter of fact, let me use terms that some of us can understand better: dogged out, used, abused, betrayed or treated like we have spiritual AIDS or leprosy. And, we probably want to go through independently, but because independency is the work of the flesh. It will attract resentment, bitterness, anger, envy, jealously, etc.

This is where satan does his greatest work. By this time he is so desperate that he will offer you everything—when you are burnt out and feel you cannot press any further. Ask anyone that's ever compromised anything, they probably were burnt out, lonely, frustrated, and at the point of feeling that everyone was against them, or perhaps they just saw a quicker way to accomplish a task. Compromise looks attractive when we are wounded. The greatest lesson I learned through my own personal pain is not to carry over any emotional pain, but carry over the victory of overcoming my pain. People are more vulnerable to compromise when emotionally wounded, and I speak from experience. Because of my own emotional pain, I compromised and fell into most of my pits.

Jesus did not bring over into the resurrection any emotional pain that He may have felt while bearing His cross and hanging on that tree. No memory of the wounds or the scars of being beaten; nor the scourging or the whipping; nor the piercing in the side, the scars upon His forehead from the thorns, the heart broken, the mental dis- tress or the anguish He felt at Calvary. As a matter of fact, let me say the only physical wound that He brought over was evidence that He came down off the cross. Other than that, He brought over the power and glory of the resurrection; He brought over power, love and a sound mind; victory and the boldness of the Holy Spirit that can go down to hell and tell the devil *because I did not compromise you must give me the keys back to the Kingdom of Heaven.* In Hades, He took the Kingdom's of the world back by victory from the hands of the enemy. He took back the life taken from Adam in Eden because He willingly gave His up. Jesus took it without compromise. The image and likeness of God that Adam compromised Jesus restored into the Kingdom without compromise.

The only thing that you and I should want to carry over from our experience is the power of the resurrection and the victory of our new life, so that our children and their children and their children's children, and those we mentor, will not have to experience the struggles and failures that you and I did. Yes, show them the scars in your hands and the wounds in your side as a testimony of where you've been, not as a testimony that you are still a bleeding victim. Say to them, "Without these scars, I would not be the man or woman of God that I am."

I believe when the disciples were shut up in that room because they feared that the Jewish Sanhedrin were coming to get them next, Jesus came in and revealed His wounds for two reasons. The first reason was to say "I can feel your pain" and the second, "I overcame this without compromise."

When you go through as much pain and suffering that some of us have gone through, you have a greater appreciation and gratitude for the cross, and it becomes very hard to compromise your position you have inherited in God through Christ. The main point of this chapter is that mentors must learn to fight and resist temptations of any form, so that those we mentor can know how to resist the devil. The lust of the flesh, the lust of the eyes, and the pride of life have been for years the only three avenues the enemy has had to tempt you.

He is coming through one way or the other. There are no other venues. These three areas reveal independency and self- provision, pride, arrogance, and compromise. These things, from Genesis 3:6, to Matthew 4:1-11, to 1 John 2:15-17 even unto now until the Lord's final appearance, will be the reasons why men and women fail and cannot prevail over the power, principalities, and the rulers of the darkness of this world, and over spiritual wickedness in high places. There is no resistance.

We waste too much time teaching twelve step programs to obtain victory and to resist the devil. There are no ten or twelve step programs—just Christ. Many have lost their confidence, and when you lose it in one area, I believe you lose it in all areas. Confidence is a mindset: confidence in yourself, people, places, and things will always lead to failure. Your abilities lay hidden in Christ; you are not invincible or invulnerable. No more depending on self. Don't let pride stand in your way any longer—no more compromise. James 4:7-10 says: *Submit yourselves therefore to God. Resist the devil, and he will flee from you. Draw nigh to God, and he will draw nigh to you. Cleanse your hands, ye sinners; and purify your hearts, ye double minded. Be afflicted, and mourn, and weep: let your laughter be turned to mourning, and your joy to heaviness. Humble your- selves in the sight of the Lord, and he shall lift you up.*

No programs. I tell people the easiest way you can resist the devil is to just submit to the Lord. If you submit to the Lord, you don't not have to resist the devil, it happens automatically. Our present and future mentors must understand the importance of submitting to and trusting God through the wilderness areas of ministry and during our encounters with satan.

Integrity is knowing who you are; you have nothing to prove to yourself, the enemy or anyone else around you. Wherefore, let him that thinks he stands take heed lest he fall. *"There hath no temptation taken you but such as is com- mon to man: but God is faithful, who will not suffer you to be tempted above that ye are able; but will with the temptation also make a way to escape, that ye may be able to bear it"* (1 Corinthians 10:13).

Let's always remember David, for he carried over all his pain and torment into the lives of not only his children, but also into the lives of those that sat under his leadership. He was a mighty man of valor, and a great king whose heart was after God, but he suffered from an unhealed heart. His sons and his servants suffered because he did not refuse to carry it over.

This is a moment to take some time to do a self-examination of your heart and really see what is hibernating within it. What will produce in your children? What will you produce in those that you mentor? Will they be a reproduction of your scorned past or will they be a product of the life of an individual whose heart has been healed by the power and resurrection of Jesus Christ? The most important thing that we need to consider is that it is not about us, it is about those who are coming behind us.

It must have hurt David intensely when he was confronted by God through his prophet, Nathan. I remember when the Lord really touched my life and healed my heart for real. I spent a day reliving some events that took place in my life, and I began to think about my torment. Then I thought about all the people that have suffered because of it. I mean I will never get a chance to say I am sorry to some because they have gone on to be with the Lord. But I became burdened because sometimes you really do not know how what you do affects a person as long as you are marinating in your own torment. Somehow you become an emotionalist. So, because of my past and because of what I put others through, everyone else reaped the benefits of being mentored and not tormented.

This is the point where you refuse to carry your own torment into another person's life, and realize that everything that you have overcome and endured was for a purpose. I like what the Apostle

Paul says in Romans 8:28-29a: *"And we know that all things work together for good to them that love God, to them who are the called according to his purpose. For whom he did foreknow, he also did predestinate to be conformed to the image of his Son."*

I love verse twenty-eight because I understand that all things are working for my good, even when it doesn't feel like it, because I love God and am called according to His purpose. But there is nothing that awakens the spirit more than to know that I was predestined to be conformed to the image of His son. What that means to me is that if I was predestined to be conformed to the image of His son, then all my trials and tribulations were predestined as well. Even when I was being tormented or suffering, He had a way of escape planned before I was even aware that I was hurting. Knowing that gives me peace and a comfort because a way of escape has already being prepared for the things I have not yet encountered.

As a mentor grips his or her pain and your suffering, they become the means that He uses to transform you into the image of His Son, because it brings you to the point of Jabez: *Lord enlarge my territory, put your hands on me that evil cannot harm and that I might not cause pain.* It brings you to the point of crying out that His Kingdom come; and if not, it should, especially for those who are mentoring or are in any area of leadership.

You should be concerned about what you bring with you in the crossover, because lives are at stake. Bridge-builder, as you build your bridge to connect generations you are crossing over, what are you carrying with you to the other side? Before you make your journey to the other side, do a self-examination and make sure that what you are taking over are the things that are necessary for pushing and mentoring of lives into destiny and purpose, and not those things that will build self-motives, test God, or compromise his word. REFUSE, to carry it over.

Chapter Five
Forgive, Forget, and "Move Forward

We are dealing with generations that have produced nothing but torment in the lives of those they mentor, the effect of which is anger, bitterness, and resentment. These are causes for unforgiveness. One of our greatest downfalls as people is the power to forgive. This goes beyond forgiving the tormentor that committed the offense; in most cases we need to forgive even ourselves.

We can never operate in the healing ministry of the Christ or the Father's Kingdom until we learn how to effectively operate in the power of forgiveness. Looking at Luke 23:34a it states, *"Then said Jesus, Father forgive them; for they know not what they do."* We see the Kingdom operating here in the power of forgiveness, coming out of the mouth of the greatest Mentor that ever lived. I don't believe that any of us can identify with the pain, suffering, and torment Christ underwent to ensure that an entire world was reconciled back to God. He was CRUCIFIED! I would rather experience any other type of death than crucifixion.

He was scourged, spat on, refused, rejected, beaten beyond measure with a whip that ripped opened at least a half inch every time it hit His flesh. He was pierced in the side. He was mocked not just by those before Him on the ground, but even by one next to Him on the cross. They pressed a crown of thorns on His forehead. He was betrayed by those who walked closely with Him. Who can bare such pain today? The only words that came out of His mouth were *"Father, forgive them for they know not what they do."*

Forgiveness had to be released before the power of the resurrection could be. Hearts that are bound by bitterness, anger, resentment, and regret are hearts that have not experienced true forgiveness. Mentors who wrestle with unforgiveness are mentors that are the most ineffective mentors ever. Luke 4:18-19 states:

> *The Spirit of the Lord is upon me, because he hath anointed me to preach the gospel to the poor; he hath sent me to heal the brokenhearted, to preach deliverance to the captives, and recovering of sight to the blind, to set at liberty them that are bruised. To preach the acceptable year of the Lord.*

Here you have the ministry of Christ that is given to every mentor. The ministry of the mentor gives the richness of the Kingdom to poor lives, heals broken hearts, sets free those who are in bondage, gives sight to those who are spiritually blind, and sets at liberty to those that are bruised. Unforgiveness dampers that anointing; it is a type of bondage, a blindness, a bruise. It's brokenness, and the only time you have power over something is when you overcome it yourself.

If you have not been restored, even though you have the word knowledge of restoration, your ability to move effectively in it is tainted by your unforgiving heart. For you to say, "I can forgive you, but cannot forget what you are doing," is setting yourself up for failure. Whenever you say you forgive and don't forget, all you are doing is pushing it to the back and saying I will deal with it later.

When you see the who, what, when, where or why, you dig up that old experience again; so for we, who consider ourselves mentors, it is imperative that the ministry of forgiveness is "first" operating in our lives. You know what I really believe? I believe the root of unforgiveness, resentfulness, bitterness, and anger is not so much in the offense. We have been warned by Christ that offenses would come. Look at Luke 17:1-6. As He continues to teach on forgiveness, He says:

> *...It is impossible but that offenses will come: but woe unto him, through whom they come! It were better for him that a millstone were hanged about his neck, and he cast into the sea, than that he should offend one of these little ones. Take heed to yourselves: If thy brother trespass against thee, rebuke him; and if he repent, forgive him. And if he trespass against thee seven times in a day, and*

> *seven times in a day turn again to thee, saying, I repent; thou shalt forgive him. And the apostles said unto the Lord, Increase our faith. And the Lord said, If ye had faith as a grain of mustard seed, ye might say unto this sycamine tree, Be thou plucked up by the root, and be thou planted in the sea; and it should obey you.*

Forgiveness, it is one of the most misunderstood teachings. This teaching is so critical for every torn-mentor or those being mentored to understand. The first thing Jesus teaches is that offenses will come that will make it impossible for you to avoid being offended. Paul says in Romans 8:36: *"As it is written, For thy sake we are killed all the day long; we are accounted as sheep for the slaughter."* Being in Christ, we take the chance of being offended. Jesus says that whoever offends one of these little ones, it would be better for a millstone to be tied around his neck and be dropped to the bottom of the sea. I believe little ones can refer to those that are immature in the faith, and this warning was unto those that have been around for a long time! Do you know how many people have been offended because of religion?

The first principle that Jesus teaches about forgiveness is rebuke. He says if your brother offends you, rebuke him. The word rebuke only means to admonish. Admonish means to warn, to reprove mildly or to exhort. In other words, make the individual aware of their offense against you and exhort on Jesus' warning about offense. Some people are not even aware that they've offended you.

Mentors, because of your offense and your own torment, you probably regularly offend those you mentor. When we understand this principle fully, we can prevent potential bitterness, anger, or resentment from setting in. Now, I realize that it is not the actual offenses that cause the bitterness or resentment, it is the fact that the offender does not take ownership of the offense committed, or even acknowledge it. And when you do not acknowledge your wrongful act towards another through repentance, you are communicating to them that it is alright for you to hurt me. That is the root of bitterness, because you feel as though what you did to me was okay.

The truth about unforgiveness, however, is that the offended is still partially responsible for his or her offense because you did not rebuke the offender. Jesus' teachings says that when someone hurts you, whether knowingly or unknowingly, and they realize it is wrong, say something about it. Warn them, because if there is any type of conviction in their life they will repent. Offended child of God, it is completely up to you to approach them and recall to their attention what God's word says about offenders. Tell them what they just did or said to you hurt you. If they will not take acknowledgement for it, make them.

REPENT

The second principle Jesus teaches about forgiveness is repent. He says rebuke him, and if he repents, forgive him (Luke 17:3b). This is one of the primary reasons why most people hold on to unforgiveness: because there is no repentance. The offender does not take ownership for their offense, and "this" is greater at times than the offense itself.

As Christians, we sometimes behave as if just because another Christian offends us, they must automatically come to us and apologize. According to Jesus, teaching a person to repent towards you is not required where they are not admonished (made aware of the offense). Just as you are not required to forgive an individual that does not repent or ask for forgiveness, the same principle for forgiveness applies, whether it is us towards God, or whether it us towards one another. And that principle is this: If you ask God to forgive you He will forgive.

You cannot just live your sinful lives without God and take an attitude that assumes that just because He is the sovereign of the world and merciful, that He automatically forgives. Just as you had to approach God in repentance and ask for His forgiveness, if you offend anyone you have to approach them the same way God requires you to approach Him; and the same is likewise if someone offends you. Now, this does not mean that you feed on that offense and that because of it you have the right to harbor bitterness, anger and resentment.

There are some steps that you need to take as a Christian to keep your heart from being invaded by those spirits. And that is prayer and fasting. In communicating with God, He will communicate with you on how to handle it. One definition of the word fast means to be firmly fixed, so that you are not easily freed. This is why I believe fasting should be a way of life and that we should fast daily for some amount of time, so that we can stay firmly fixed while God deals with our tormentor and adversary. Remember, offenses should not be assumed, and apologies should not be automatically expected without first calling the matter to the attention of the offender.

Some mentors are still torn over issues that happened years ago, and they cannot get their ministries, personal lives, or Kingdom relationships together because unforgiveness has found a home in their hearts. They cannot produce the fruitfulness of the Kingdom in their offspring. How many of your tormentors have you actually rebuked or made aware that they even offended you? I harbored anger and bitterness for years, waiting for people to come and apologize to me, until I read this text through the eyes of the Kingdom. Some folks where surprised when they found out that they actually hurt me. They expressed extreme and genuine Kingdom repentance, and it released me. The thing Jesus teaches on forgiveness is that no matter how many times they offended you, if they come repenting, whether it is seven times a day or every day for your entire life, you are to forgive them. Notice the reply of the apostles in Luke 17:5: *"Lord, increase our faith."* This verse made me laugh because out of all the things they could have asked the Lord to increase their faith for, it was for the faith to forgive someone who constantly torments them.

When someone continually hurts you, it eventually becomes hard to endure. Just to shift for a moment, because even though this book is for the mentor, there are many families, relationships, and marriages that have been torn apart because of continued abuse or torment. Mental, emotional, or even physical abuse—how do you continue to forgive after years and years of constant torment? One can only do this through the resurrection power of Christ. Unforgiveness has stood in the way of great mentors being successful in releasing the Kingdom of God in the lives of those that are coming behind them. Unforgiveness will cause you to lose your salt!

Since I can remember, my whole life has been built upon torment and tormenting. I could never get over it. As I said earlier, even as a pastor, I could not pastor correctly or even mentor effectively. Bitterness and anger destroyed most of my relationships. It was not that I was just angry and bitter; when something was done to me, I will hold it for weeks, months, and even years. Unforgiveness stopped my ability to love. It prevented the presence of the Lord from flowing and changing my life, even lives in the ministry. My wife at the time and I used to bring our unloving, unforgiving, bitter, resentful selves to the Temple. I'd preach, and I mean preach the word, and she would sit there with her attitude. Pretty soon it killed the ministry. Members left and eventually she did too. She had her own struggles in her life since childhood that she needed to overcome. My reason for saying this is unforgiving hearts will kill the move of God. The torn-mentor has to learn to forgive, forget, and move forward.

FORGET

I hear so many people say they have forgiven, but have not forgotten; I really find that to be an untrue statement. Forgetting is the center of forgiveness. If one cannot forgive, chances are they have not forgotten. When you have not forgotten, certain encounters in your new experiences will remind you of past torments. Isaiah 65:16b states: *"Because the former troubles are forgotten, and because they are hid from mine eyes."* In true repentance, there is no more remembering of the former troubles. When genuine repentance takes place, there should be no more memory of it. Once we have allowed forgiveness to take place, allow it to work so the heart is totally healed. Moving forward in Christ means forgetting those things which are behind. Paul says in Philippians 3:13b-14: *"But this one thing I do, forgetting those things which are behind, and reaching forth unto those things which are before, I press toward the mark for the prize of the high calling of God in Christ Jesus."*

I like what the Apostle says here. He says three words that are very important: *forgetting, reaching,* and *pressing.* I had to meditate on these words before I understood what the apostle Paul was saying. He was saying he must forget everything that is behind him and reach for the things which are before him. The word before means in advance or ahead of. Then he says he has to press. Anytime you are reaching for something new or something that God has moved in front or ahead of you that He has ordained, the things that are behind you can hinder you reaching and actually grabbing those things which are before you. This is why Paul says I PRESS, because sometimes you've got to press or force your way through those things you are trying to forget or that are behind you.

> Let us consider Hebrews 12:1: *Wherefore seeing we also are com- passed about with so great a cloud of witnesses, let us lay aside every weight, and the sin which doth so easily beset us, and let us run with patience the race that is set before us.*

A weight is a mass, as bending and bulging by its load; it is a burden or hindrance. Many mentors have overcome sin—it is more so the weight that affects them. Not forgetting the former things can be the biggest weight ever. Weights will affect how well you run; they can slow down the process. The word "before," as mentioned in Philippians 3:13, is the same for Hebrews 12:1. It means to move in advance of, or in front of. The weight of not forgetting your past and harboring unforgiveness can stop you in your tracks, preventing you from moving forward to those things that are in advance of you; and also those you are to help move into the things that lay in advance for them.

Just being honest, some torments are hard to forget about. But can you imagine how hard it would be if God took the same attitude most of us take when it comes to forgiving and forgetting? We would probably not be able to lay hold of any promise. Just imagine for a moment if God remembered and held on to every offense that you committed before Him. His mercy endures forever. Mercy is an act of forgiving and forgetting.

You cannot give cheerfully in bondage, whether it is money, time, love, or service rendered. God loves a cheerful giver. God honors your attitude of giving more than He honors your giving. *"Blessed are the merciful for they shall obtain mercy"* (Matthew 5:7). The Greek meaning of the word merciful is compassionate, benevolent, involving thought and action so to give not grudgingly, which means that you are genuine in your giving. You really cannot give those you mentor anything unless you have received it.

Let me say that most people who have a desire to impart into someone's life and have not been released from unforgiveness and not forgetting, will only release frustration during the impartation process. They will probably find some fault with the person that they are mentoring or some reason to give up, when it is really not them at all, but it is you. *"...Forgetting those things which are behind, and reaching forth unto those things which are before, I press toward the mark for the prize of the high calling of God in Christ Jesus"* (Philippians 3:13b-14).

The cost of moving forward into greater things will always be the letting go of the lesser things. Moving forward, mentor, is important for you because as you move forward you are bringing those you mentor right along with you. Your life just might be the before (things that are moved in advance of) for somebody else. To move forward might cause you to have to press. The Greek word for "press" means to flee, to pursue, ensue or follow after, which gives us an indication that there is something waiting ahead for you.

God will never encourage us to move forward from where we are unless He has something greater in place, not only in the physical but also in thought, heart, and spirit. Most people move forward in the natural aspects of life, but can never move forward mentally or emotionally. In the moving forward process, you have to make up in your mind and emotions that you refuse to carry this over. Many of us will spend years in Gilgal, which means rolling the reproach away or a place where you are just camping out until you allow God to circumcise your heart, because God will not allow you to carry over the reproach from where you have been into where you are going.

The moving forward process requires us to move out of something into something else. I believe that the greatest reason Jesus did not halt and kept moving forward, forgetting every bad experience that ever happened to Him—even the experience that He was undergoing during His journey to the tree—was because He understood the importance of His life. Jesus was determined to carry our afflictions and die with them so that we could reap the benefits of His power and resurrection.

If we did a replay of the offenses that Jesus underwent during His ministry, we would have to come to the conclusion that if anyone had the right to give up, He did. I believe He was not there in the multitude while He hung there, but I believe that the only reason Jesus did not get off the wooden planks and lay His cross down was because of the plea of the thief that hung next to Him: *"Lord remember me when you come into your Kingdom"* (Luke 23:42).

This was no normal cry, but this was an earnest plea enquiring, in other words, "Lord, if you do not remember anyone else, for my sake, please walk it out and hang there for me. I need you in the power of your resurrection." Jesus understood that His death was important for the life of others. Hear the many that are crying for you to endure your cross, die to your experiences, and move forward. Your recovery is so important that you have to let go of the bitterness and resentment of your past. Go and die to your cross.

There has been so much torment inflicted upon this generation, ranging from rape, rejection, sodomy, child molestation, etc. These scars are the result of mental and emotional abuse, and individuals are dramatically heart struck. The aftermath of it all is unforgiveness. The Body of Christ has to take the leading position in releasing the spirit of forgiveness in our regions. It will be...

> *...like the precious ointment upon the head, that ran down upon the beard, even Aaron's beard: that went down to the skirts of his garments. As the dew of Hermon, and as the dew that descended upon the mountains of Zion: for there the LORD commanded the blessing, even life for evermore.* —Psalm 133:2-3

Forgiveness is the interlude for unity. Whenever forgiveness is unleashed on the Body, it will build a fortress against division and separation—securing unity in its place. Whatever flows down from the head covers the rest of the body. Mentor, you represent Aaron. Whatever flows down your beard and off the skirts of your garment spills over into the lives you mentor; and, God forbid if you're pouring out unforgiveness. The worst thing you can do to yourself, child of God, is to continue living as though everything is well within you. Even though you manifest on the outside healing and physically you appear to people to be doing well, there is an emotional and mental healing that needs to take place.

This generation needs the ministry of the Christ that is waiting to flow through a forgiving heart, not the misery of your crisis that is bound by an unforgiving heart. Forgive, forget and move forward, and bring those that are coming behind you into the place of rest, restoration, and release. My God! I just got excited thinking about the level of power that God would unleash upon your life if you walk in that forgiving love.

Unforgiveness is standing in the way of you becoming an effective mentor. When we are children, our hearts are at their best. We are born trusting and loving at full capacity—loving and trusting any and everybody because our infant hearts are full. But I believe as we grow and begin to have experiences, every bad experience steals a little bit of our heart; and now at twenty, thirty, forty, fifty and sixty our hearts are less loving and trusting. This makes it hard

THE CRY OF A GENERATION:
Forgive, Forget, and Move Forward

to deal with people that remind us of our tormentors. We become prejudice against those we choose to deal with.

Believe it or not, this is the result of an unforgiving heart Imagine for a moment that your life at the age you are now, was so wonderful—never had a heart attack, and your level of love and trust has never been tampered with—you would probably love and trust any and every one. I believe when we allow the Lord to really deal with the issue of an unforgiving heart and cleanse us from all the anger, bitterness and resentment, we can embrace people the way God embraces us.

When God replenishes us, it should show us being clothed with that humility that our Lord and Savior wore. The level of love for God's people should increase as we decrease, even the love for our tormentors. That will be our greatest challenge: to forgive those that continue to hurt us. Jesus' pouring of His life into ours brings our hearts back to their full capacity.

There are people who are reading this book whose entire life has been built upon one tormenting experience after the next; and your heart and ability to love and receive love, has been torn by that bitter root of unforgiveness. But it is critical in this hour that you grab onto God's forgiveness for your own life, and even the lives of your tormentors. It is time that you confront the tormentors of your past and let them know that they have hurt you; whether it is a father, mother, uncle, grandfather, family friend, pastor, teacher, husband, or wife. It is time for you to have some closure and move forward, because there is so much that God has in store for your life.

Your experiences and healing is the answer for the cry of this generation. Your voice needs to be heard. So, as I bring this chapter to a close, I am led to have a word of prayer with you that the Lord will strengthen you in this capacity:

__Father God in heaven in Jesus' name__, we approach your throne NOW with boldness, that we may obtain mercy and find grace to help in this time of need. You have given us the keys to the Kingdom of Heaven. Whatever we bind on earth is bound in Heaven, and whatever we loose on earth is loosed in Heaven. We bind the tormenting stronghold of unforgiveness that has set up a fortresses against your power, glory, and will in this person. They have struggled with this stronghold long enough, but today we speak to this mountain and command it to be removed in Jesus' name. They want to flow in your power and love, and walk in your spirit. Reproduce in them, Father, your image and your likeness that they may exercise the character of your Kingdom and walk with your authority and power. Today they are taking authority over their mind, heart, and soul; and Father you release them from this bondage. We confess that they are healed and have been made whole. Your resurrection power has enabled them to forgive, forget, and move forward. I speak this by the power of your Word, in Jesus' name, Amen.

Chapter Six

Mentoring After The Father's Heart

One critical thing we must understand, comprehend and consider for those who have mentoring ability, is that when the people who are qualified to mentor refuse to mentor, those who are not qualified will. The majority of mentors we have that are not qualified and are willing are greater than the number of the qualified but unwilling prospective mentors. This is because the qualified are not reproducing; they have not allowed anyone to come inside their matrix.

Mentors need to be shaped and designed after the Father's heart, and I am referring to God. What I mean by after the Father's heart, is to be in pursuit of God's desire, purpose, plans, and longings. God's heart should be the guiding force or influence that provokes every mentor's heart. The original meaning of the word *after* is a primitive root word which means the hind part, after that, behind or in pursuit of. The reason I make mention of these words is because a mentor, especially on the Kingdom level, must understand that a foundation has already been laid, and we are to follow and build upon that foundation.

God has laid a foundation through Christ, establishing character, attitude, personality and the heart of the Father, which has been painted perfectly in the person of Christ. We are in the hind part of that foundation. We are behind and in pursuit of the established order. A mentor that is after the heart of the Father will follow the established standard. There are mentors who are mentors by nature and have no problem following a standard or model that has been set. Then you have mentors who are the product of their experiences whose wills have not been broken yet. These mentors do not have the character, attitude, personality, or heart of the Father. Mentors that are not after the Father's heart usually end up shipwrecked, and wreck the lives of others as they drive their damaged vessel to and fro through the hearts of the hungry and thirsty.

Now you have another type of mentor, and these are handpicked by God himself. Pulled out of their own torments, they were shaped, designed, and molded by the hand of God. These have been anointed and are characterized by godly traits. God produced Himself in their character, attitude, and personality. He took away the stony heart and gave them a heart of flesh—a heart that can be dealt with. He poured Himself into that earthen vessel, concealing Himself inside someone who is sensitive to the spirit and who captured and is willing to learn and understand the heart of the Father, and willing to allow the Father to operate through their heart. This is the mentor that will be successful.

I used to think that people who have had the grooming and training made the best of everything, but my thoughts are now different. I believe now that those of us who have lacked become more than those who have not, because people who have not had a mentor or father know how it feels to be without, and we tend to give people what we ourselves longed for but never had.

Looking at Jesus' example, the perfect picture or model of the Father's heart in the flesh, He gives us the ability because of what He carried over into the resurrection. That energy and source of power and authority that was in Him is what He produces in us. We can find a picture of the Father's heart in the attributes of God, also known as the Beatitudes, found in the 5th chapter of St. Matthew. He's poor in spirit, a mourner, meek, hungry and thirsty after righteousness. He's merciful, a peacemaker, and pure in heart.

Many who don't have the Father's heart do not have it because they are not in pursuit of it. Jesus gives us in Matthew 16:24b-26, what I believe is a closer look at the Father's heart in function. He says:

> *If any man will come after me, let him deny himself, and take up his cross, and follow me. For whosoever will save his life shall lose it: and whosoever will lose his life for my sake shall find it. For what is a man profited, if he shall gain the whole world, and lose his own soul? or what shall a man give in exchange for his soul? For the*

Son of man shall come in the glory of His Father with His angels; and then He shall reward every man according to his works.

What I believe Jesus gives us here is the function of a mentor that mentors after the Father's heart, allowing the Father's ability to work through us. No man's heart, with all its hurts and pain, is so torn that God cannot repair it if given the opportunity. The spiritual heart performs the same duties to the spiritual body as the physical heart performs for the physical body. It is the life of the body, just as the physical heart is the throne upon which life itself sits. When removed from the physical body it produces death—so too is your spiritual heart. When you remove your spiritual heart out of anything it dies. And what I mean by your spiritual heart is the thoughts, the feelings, the seat of the desires, passions, affections , and impulses. The original meaning of this word is *kardia,* and it explains the heart as being so much more than an internal organ that pumps blood through the veins and arteries, spreading blood throughout the entire body so it can function properly. Your heart is also the safe haven for your emotions. Your heart is the life, and it's your heart that determines how much life remains in the body, whether it is a physical or spiritual heart.

David, after a life filled with torment in his natural and spiritual house by his spiritual Father, came to the realization that his heart was not right, even though God testified that David was a man after His own heart. David mourned for the torment that was in his heart that spilled over upon him and caused him to do to Uriah, on a greater level, what Saul did to him. It is our duty to mourn for a new heart after having our hearts drenched with torment. It is something for a man to come to the realization that his heart is torn and filled with sin, and that he should not ignore that there is need for some repairing.

Some people ignore the need for heart surgery and cover their tormented hearts in religious faces or behind their titles. In Psalm 51:1 (NKJ) David says, *"Create in me a clean heart, O God, And renew a steadfast (or a right) spirit within me."* This shows us that even in a torn and wounded heart, there is a longing for healing and closure. David was a man who suffered from a heart that was tremendously broken because of what he experienced in both his natural and spiritual father's house, and because of that he was only able to give what he had received. Though David expressed genuine repentance, even after repentance there had to be a foundation laid to maintain further reassurance of comforting. He needed a good *kenosis,* a Greek word which means an emptying out of self! And until a man receives a good kenosis, refilling of the Father's heart is impossible.

We try so hard to change our hearts without changing our thoughts. In order for a person to have stable and healthy emotions, they have to have a healthy thought life. Your mind will replay every event and experience you have had and may cause your heart to emotionally react in a particular way. I never knew just how important the condition of my heart was until I became a father, mentor, and pastor. It was not until then I began to recognize the true condition of my heart. This is funny because in my B.C. (before Christ), the condition of my heart was seen by everyone but me. Everyone else knew how I was, even when I believed that for the life I was living my heart was right.

Salvation has somehow brought me outside myself and has given me a visual of Lawrence. For the first time I realized that I have heart issues and being saved was not good enough; going to church was not good enough. There was a need that being saved and church could not fix. I needed the Christ to invade my heart and give me a revelation of the heart of God. God really started to deal with me according to the Beatitudes in Matthew 5:3-12, and also what I will call the Father's heart in action in Matthew 16:24-28.

The very first thing Jesus says to us that will help our hearts to be converted so that we can mentor after the Father's heart is in Matthew 16:24: *"If any man will come after me, let him deny himself."* Denying yourself is the key to mentoring after God's heart because the Kingdom of God is an unselfish Kingdom. To deny yourself literally means to deny your heart the rights to feed life to all those bitter, angry and hurtful feelings. It means to deny yourself the right to harbor resentment, to deny yourself according to my terms means that you do not even notice yourself.

We should come to the place where our hearts are so converted into the image and likeness of the Father's heart that we should not even notice ourselves. A friend of mine once asked a jeweler "When gold has been refined, is it refined when it comes out of the fire?" The jeweler replied, "Even when the gold comes out of the refiner's fire, it is still full of dross. All the refiner's fire does is bring to surface that which is on the inside so that it can be dealt with." When the dross surfaces, the gold is buffed and shined until the jeweler can see his reflection. So I perceived a revelation in my mind that even though we may have come out of our fiery trails, the image of the Father's heart has not been perfected in us until He can look into our hearts and see His image and likeness—this is a lifelong process.

So as long as you can look in your heart and still see a reflection of yourself, the work has not been completed. But when you get to the point where you do not even notice yourself, you are almost there. When a mentor refuses to carry his or her own heart over, they are refusing to be controlled by any past torments or selfish ambitions that might hinder the growth of the person that they are mentoring. And so when the Father's heart is working through you, you do not even notice yourself. Jesus, when He speaks He speaks in an order that is to be followed. The reason, I believe, He says deny yourself first is because <u>self</u> is the foundation for failure and destruction.

Mentors who deny their past the right to influence their hearts, can influence a world that there is life after torment! When you read the story of Joseph in Genesis, chapters 38-45, you see how Joseph, who portrays a type of Christ, had an opportunity to avenge himself when his brothers put him in a pit, which led him to being sold into slavery. He ended up in a house of lies

(Potiphar's house) which costed him his freedom, although he was eventually liberated, he denied himself the right to seek revenge against his brethren. Even when the tables were turned, and Joseph had an opportunity to do to his brothers what they did to him he did not. Amazingly, it actually broke his heart to see his brothers suffer.

The Father's heart was operating in him, even to the point where it tormented him to play the little games he played with them. We see David all through 1 Samuel have plenty of opportunity to take the life of the spiritual father that sought after his life, but David had such a heart of God that he refused. David still respected Saul as one of God's anointed. When you live a life that is based on denying yourself, you make the Kingdom of God look attractive to those you are mentoring, and to those around you as well.

CROSS-BEARING

Matthew 5:8 states: *"Blessed are the pure in heart, for they shall see God."* The Father's heart is pure, and those that seek to see His move must be pure in their hearts. Allowing self to operate in our lives, ministries, churches, etc., has always hindered us from seeing God move. Not noticing yourself will allow you to notice God. It really becomes easy to "take up your cross and follow Him" when you have denied yourself, which is the second piece of evidence that shows the Father's heart working in you.
Jesus says, "Take up your Cross." Most people who have not denied themselves will find it hard to "take up their cross." Cross-

bearing can be unbearable when self is not denied—this is when denying yourself is ineffective because it is more than taking up whatever cross it is that you have to bear.

In addition, character, attitude and personality (C.A.P.) means everything when mentoring. More people have put down their crosses only to pick them up again. I believe the reason is because the art behind cross-bearing is the denying of self; and I know to some a statement like the art of cross-bearing may sound a bit awkward, but there is an art to cross-bearing. To master the art of cross-bearing is keeping your integrity during your pain and suffering, and realizing that the purpose behind your cross-bearing is for everyone that's coming behind you.

I believe the greatest reason why cross-bearing is hard for most mentors is because we confuse the actual cross for the plus sign that was strapped to our Lord's back. That was just extra weight. Acts 5:30 says: *"The God of our fathers raised up Jesus whom you murdered by hanging on a tree."* Let us deal with this cross thing for a moment. The meaning of the word cross is any design or mark made by two intersecting lines or bars; to intersect or to oppose; any trouble or affliction. We know that to intersect means to cut, to oppose, to contend with or resist. According to the Greeks, the word *cross* means to stand, to bear or carry. When applied it means to endure or uphold. The picture of the plus sign on Jesus' back was to intersect Him from dying on the tree. He struggled to carry those two planks of wood up Calvary because the actual cross He bore was us. He had to die to His own pain and agony in order to carry ours and die, according to God's plan. Now listen very carefully as I say this again: we were His cross because it was man that tried to intersect and opposed His purpose. It was man that afflicted and troubled Him. But at the same time He had to bear, uphold and endure, even when we contended and resisted Him.

I hope I am not being too deep here, but at the same token, as He bore the affliction for us, we are to bear affliction for each other—even when we are opposed and troubled by those we are in relationships with. Cross- bearing, in a sense, is nothing more than an intersection while you are pressing towards the mark for the prize of a higher call. What happens when the stuff that you are enduring for and upholding starts to afflict, trouble, contend, or resist you? In some cases, many have put the cross down. Also even in another sense, when dealing with the word "oppose," there are some spiritual things that come to oppose during our cross bearing phase, that can make cross bearing a strain on the mental and emotional levels as well.

Some crosses and causes of crosses include: ministry, marriage, sickness, finances, family, relationships, and business abuse of every kind. And causes of these crosses are pastors, ministers, mentors, husbands, wives, sons, daughters, friends, sisters, or brothers. Know if you deny yourself the rights to get emotionally involved or mentally distressed about your cross experiences, you can take up your cross and bear it with the C.A.P. on character, attitude and personality. Mentors that usually end up shipwrecked and wrecking the lives of those they mentor are mentors that cannot take up their cross. Cross-bearing is easy when you are in pursuit of the Father's heart.

The third example for mentoring after the Father's heart is following the example of Christ. Jesus says in Matthew 16:24: *"...Follow me."* I believe the most damaging thing a mentor can do to a person is mislead them or run ahead of Christ. In the Kingdom, if we are going to preach, teach, and evangelize Christ and the Kingdom of God, we need to teach those we mentor to follow His example and not our own. Jesus was the Father's heart in the flesh and still is the Father's heart that lives in us, through His resurrection and our confession. I almost made the biggest mistake in the early years of my pastoral call by patterning what God called me to do after religion, organization, and a bunch of rules and regulations. I was preaching Christ and unconsciously teaching people to follow and serve an organization.

What does Christ mean when He says follow me? Considering His life as being the example for the type of life we should live in God's Kingdom, I believe we should pay attention not just to His character, attitude and personality, but also how He handled people in His mentoring. To follow means to be in the same way, to accompany (especially as a disciple) to go with. The following of Christ is in relation to the Kingdom then, now and the future. We are to follow His example as if He still physically lives, which in actuality He does because He lives in us. I like what 1 Peter 2:21-24 in the Message version of the Bible says:

> *This is the kind of life you've been invited into, the kind of life Christ lived. He suffered everything that came His way so you would know that it could be done, and also know how to do it, step-by-step. He never did one thing wrong. Not once said anything amiss. They called him every name in the book and he said nothing back. He suffered in silence, content to let God set things right. He used his servant body to carry our sins to the Cross so we could be rid of sin, free to live the right way. His wounds became your healing.*

This is what Christ meant when He said follow me; our wounds should be healing, instead of us being in torment for those we mentor. The NKJ says in 1 Peter 2:21, *"For to this you were called, because Christ also suffered for us, leaving us an example, that you should follow His steps:"* Now let us understand that Christ still remains a few steps ahead us. To *follow* means to accompany, not to run ahead of. I believe too many mentors are trying to run ahead of Christ, trying to operate in an office that Christ Himself does not fully occupy yet. He is High Priest, functioning as mediator and advocate; He is not reigning as King yet (Hebrews 2:14-18; 4:14- 16). We are not called to reign and drive the devil off the earth, we are called to follow Christ's earthly ministry while He acts as our High Priest. What Christ was when He walked the earth was transferred to us after His ascension; and what He did during His earthly ministry we do it to an even greater degree. In our mentoring after the Father's heart we should coach and advise those we mentor into overcoming these sorts of obstacles. We cannot teach people how to overcome pain and suffering, but we can coach and advise them through it as we ourselves follow Christ's example.

Right now, we should be teaching that we are more than conquerors, and we have power over scorpions and serpents and over all the power of the enemy, and that nothing can hurt us. These are words that came out of Jesus Christ's own mouth, in Luke 10:19. This is the same example that Jesus exercised during His earthly ministry; for He was more than a conqueror, and He exercised dominion over powers and principalities.

We witness cross prevention tactics in the wilderness in Matthew 4:1-11, to prevent Jesus from bearing His cross; and we witness cross intervention when He hangs on the plus sign to intersect the fulfillment of death. We also see rejection, false accusations, name calling, and betrayal between these two events. But at the same time we see the humility, patience, and endurance He exercised. This is what it means to follow Christ! Oh, my goodness.

Imagine never having Him as an example to follow, and instead seeing some of the other examples we had in our lives. Personally speaking, after witnessing how some of those who mentored me handled suffering, I am glad I knew about a savior named Jesus and that I could read through the word of God to see how He handled Himself during some of the most difficult periods in His life. I probably would have perished if I followed an organization, religion, man, or some other source. We are followers of Christ and there is no other example to follow.

The fourth example of mentoring after the Father's heart is having the ability to give up or exchange your life. Jesus says in Matthew 16:25, *"...Whosoever will save his life shall lose it: and whosoever will lose his life for my sake shall find it."* What does life mean to you? Or, what is your life? There is a distinct difference when it comes to understanding life according to the Father's heart and your own, because the question would come to mind: what type of life are you imparting into the lives of those you mentor?

In the beginning of this book, I stated that one of the meanings for mentor is the emptying of life from one vessel into the next. Is the life that you are pouring into after the Father's heart, or your own? We often try to hold to certain parts of our life that we obtained in the B.C. (before Christ) that are dear to us. I do not believe a person can ever fully understand the life we are called to live through Christ until he completely lets go of the life he had before Christ.

Mentoring becomes complicated on a Kingdom level when you try to impart your life into someone else's, instead of the life of Christ. Imagine your will, your desires, your value systems, being emptied into a vessel—you will reproduce another you. Our outlook on life or what life means to us comes from our experiences. I really do not believe that this particular statement is referring to the physical life that we live as I stated in a former chapter; but rather, the intellectual life that we live on the inside. How we think in our minds, feel in our hearts, and reason in our souls have become soul ties to most people. Life to you might defer from someone else's depending on the experiences. Our outlook on our experiences gives us a different perception of what life means to us as individuals. Your outer life is a complete picture of your thoughts and feelings—you can see what a person thinks or feels about life by the way they communicate, dress, and live. This is why someone might say to another, your life is messed up, because their appearance and communication expresses their reasoning.

Certain things we've been through become habitable and in most cases we are unconsciously aware that our lives are messed up. Good or bad, it's hard to let go of certain thoughts and feelings because over a period of time they became a part of who we are; and adjusting to something new can be a torment in itself. The heart of God is the life of the Kingdom of which every mentor that is mentoring future mentors should have. I am a firm believer that upon receiving Christ, you should receive His life as well—not just a verbal confession that He is Lord, but your life should start to express the very image of His person.

To *save* means to deliver or protect, it means to preserve from danger, loss or destruction. Jesus is only saying that if you try to preserve or protect your life, you will miss out on the life He offers. This is the immaterial life, the soul. Your soul is self-conscious and has a relationship with your mind and heart. Reasoning, I believe, takes place in the soul part of man. Your mind is world conscious, which relates to your vision. What you see is processed through your thoughts, then dialogued to your heart and soul, and finally brought to a conclusion. What happens is most people conclude to preserve the material and physical portions of life, because we are more world and self-conscious than God conscious. Less of ourselves and more of Christ is needed and should be desired when mentoring.

Mentors that mentor after the Father's heart understand the importance of letting go and stopping to protect a life that does not benefit them or even those they mentor. There are so many different mindsets that can intrude on the mindset of the Kingdom of God. To not save your life is simply to die to it, so you can find the life of Christ.

The wonderful thing about losing your life to Christ is it is not a loss or destruction—it is a gain! Paul makes an observation in Philippians 1:21: *"For to me to live is Christ, and to die is gain."* Even though Paul is actually talking about an out of body experience, I believe we can apply this to Matthew 16:25 and conclude that it is time to stop protecting the life we obtain in the flesh. There is a fleshly nature that we need to die to more so than dying physically.

The heart of the Father is not fleshly or carnal, it's holy; and if we are going to mentor the generations that are coming behind us and prepare them for the final move of God, there must be a letting go of the old and grabbing on to the new. I have one more verse I would like to leave before we go into the fifth and sixth examples of mentoring after the Father's heart. Paul says in Galatians 2:20: *"I am crucified with Christ: nevertheless I live; yet not I, but Christ liveth in me: and the life which I now live in the flesh I live by the faith of the Son of God, who loved me, and gave himself for me."* This is the life we all risk losing if we are not willing to lose our lives.

The material world has been the apple of the eye for many people. Most people's purpose for ministry is to gain the world, region, cities, and communities for selfish intent. When mentoring after the Father's heart, the center of focus should always be the Kingdom of God. From the beginning in Eden with the fall of God's first man, Adam (Genesis 3:6-7), through Jesus' wilderness experience (Matthew 4:1-11) all the way until now, we see satan's technique for trying to hinder the spreading of the gospel through the desires of the world: the lust of the flesh, the lust of the eyes, and the pride of life (1 John 2:14-17).

Gifts are for hire now. Everyone has a price attached to them. There is a greater need for anointed vessels, than for hired up. Matthew 16:26 NKJV says, *"For what profit is it to a man if he gains the whole world, and loses his own soul? Or what will a man give in exchange for his soul?"* The New Century Version says, *"It is worthless to have the whole world if they lose their souls. They could never pay enough to buy back their souls."* And The Message Bible says, *"What kind of deal is it to get everything you want but lose yourself? What could you ever trade your soul for?"*

The reason I speak of the fifth and sixth functions of the Father's heart together is because you cannot separate the two. If the truth can be told, a great majority of those that minister the gospel believe God more to provide for their material need before their spiritual need. Think of your own personal prayer lives. Is there too much time spent on petitioning God for financial increase, new cars, new houses, bigger congregations and new sanctuaries, than crying before the Lord day and night for a new and better you?

Televised celebrity Christians have made the Kingdom of God appear glamorous, and to the eyes of the generations that are up and-coming, they desire that glamorous lifestyle. They have a disposition that says if they can preach, play or sing their way into wealth, so can I. Then what you have is a Christian competitive star search—everyone is trying to out-preach, out-sing, and out-play one another. And while we are busy trying to gain the world's attention, the power of God is decreasing in our churches, and our services are becoming talent shows and auditions.

Souls are leaving the church and the souls that need to be there never make it there, because soul-winning is the least concern. The mentor is to shift the focus of those they mentor from seeing success through the eyes of the world, which is measured by one material possession, to see success through the eyes of the Kingdom of God, which is measured by overcoming the temptations of this world and exercising power and dominion over the Kingdom of darkness through righteous living. The material world will one day pass away.

Our worldly possessions are temporal. Jesus says that you can be the richest person in the world with dollars that no man can number, and it still is not enough to buy your way into eternal life. If your affection is set on things below and not on things above, you are setting yourself up to spend eternity with the devil and his angels.

The greatest blow to the Kingdom ever would be to raise a generation of leaders whose drive for ministry is to have the life of the rich and the famous. The concern should be how much of your life are you willing to give to become a Kingdom child? Are you willing to redirect your focus and attention on the Kingdom value system? We are a now generation living with the expectation to obtain the not yet Kingdom. And so mentors, the heart of the Father says build my end time army because in the Lord's final coming it's going to be the army of God that completely dismantles and overthrows the Kingdom of darkness.

There is a stern cry in the generations of today for mentors with a Father's heart—one full of compassion, concern, willingness, humility, warmth, forgiveness, brokenness, self-sacrifice, and service; not hearts full of control, contempt, pride, coldness, resentful, unforgiveness, selfishness, and rebellion. The Father's heart is gentle in correction. Out of the hearts of men proceed evil.

Most mentors need some spiritual triple by-pass surgery because of the condition of their heart.

Mentors, I strongly urge you before you impart life, make sure life has been imparted into you. Seek after the Father's heart always—pursue of His desires and passions. Your heart is so important to the Father for the sake of His future Kingdom. That is why there is double protection in Ephesians 6:14, 16. The heart has over it the breastplate of righteousness and is covered as well by the shield of faith. For the Father knows that if satan ever got control of your heart, he has control of your life. When satan is in control, mentors become tormentors.

Chapter Seven
Giving Generations What They Need

One of the greatest tragedies of our modern day in churches and communities all over the earth is that we live in such a compromising era. Righteousness does not seem to be very popular, even though salvation and righteousness is what this generation needs. But they are not getting it; they are going after and getting what they want by any other means except righteousness. It is now time to give this generation what it needs, and that is to properly advise, teach and coach them, and to help restructure their lives. When a person has experienced torment from a mentor, the restructuring of life is important so they can recognize the needs of others and lay foundation that is based upon those needs and not wants.

Isaiah 58:12b NKJV states: *"You shall raise up the foundations of many generations, and you shall be called the repairer of the breach, the restorer of the streets to dwell in."*

There's no other text that pierces my heart like that verse, with regard to living out the example of a concerned Kingdom Citizen. We briefly discussed this text in an earlier chapter, but I feel it is so significant to us right now. We look at generations and cultures, and the changes that have been made; and we build and structure Christ around those changes, making him look like them so he can appear attractive. We should build generations and cultures around him.

Even though I am Afro-American, and my heritage is probably rooted in Africa, who really knows the true history. My culture is Kingdom and we do things a lot differently on this side. Our tastes and cravings are different, and that is just how I view things. The Kingdom of God is a culture within itself, with its own structure.

A culture is nothing more than the act of developing the intellectual and moral faculties by educating. It is expert care and training, or for simple terminology, the customary beliefs, social forms and material traits of a racial, religious, or social group. So one of the most important things that mentors must be careful about is that we don't mix and mingle Kingdom culture with earthly culture. We live and operate according to another system of beliefs, and because we are trying to convert the earth, we must mentor those we mentor to stand out, not blend in.

We cannot look at this generation and say we are going to give them a Jay-Z, 50 Cent, Rick Ross or hip-hop Christ; or just because they cry out we want Barabbas does not mean we give them Barabbas. We have to give them what they need and not what they want. Mentors that mentor outside the Father's heart produce more leaders that are secularly oriented than Kingdom; we call them Manassehs. The Bible says in 2 Kings 21:1-6, 9:

> *Manasseh was twelve years old when he began to reign, and reigned fifty and five years in Jerusalem. And his mother's name was Hephzibah. And he did that which was evil in the sight of the Lord, after the abominations of the heathen, whom the Lord cast out before the children of Israel. For he built up again the high places which Hezekiah his father had destroyed; and he reared up altars for Baal, and made a grove, as did Ahab king of Israel; and worshipped all the host of heaven, and served them. And he built altars in the house of the Lord, of which the Lord said, In Jerusalem will I put my name. And he built altars for all the host of heaven in the two courts of the house of the Lord. But they hearkened not: and Manasseh seduced them to do more evil than did the nations whom the Lord destroyed before the children of Israel. And he made his son pass through the fire, and observed times, and used enchantments, and dealt with familiar spirits and wizards: he wrought much wickedness in the sight of the Lord, to provoke Him to anger.*

Can you imagine a generation that cries out we want Barabbas and Manasseh, then turns around and gives it to them! This generation lacks structure, strength and salvation; these are the most important elements that this generation and every generation preceding needs. Structure, strength, and salvation help overcome the double-mindedness that swarms the mentors of this age.

Now as you read this chapter I am personalizing it to you, because you are important for the final finale—the Lord's final coming. Because God has set you over the nations and over the Kingdoms, you must begin to root out and pull down, destroy and overthrow, build and plant. You shall build up the foundations of many generations and you shall be called the repairer of the breach, the restorer of streets to dwell in (Isaiah 58:12b).

I really do not want to appear as though I am preaching, but I believe this is a source of spreading the gospel and this is a great opportunity for me to MENTOR—to do some advising, teaching, and coaching. Isaiah made mention of the three key elements that are needed for today's mentors. The first of these three is *structure*, of which we have been stressing the importance of throughout this book. There are so many different meanings for the word, but one stands out to me and that is the arrangement of particles or parts in a substance, body or organization; of parts as dominated by the general character of the whole. And in this case, it is the Kingdom of God. Now I am going to divert briefly from my call and become a theologian for a minute because the word *substance* is very important. It characterizes the particles or parts that are the essential nature or the ultimate reality that underlies all outward manifestations and change. Everything about mentoring on a Kingdom level points back to Christ. He is the missing substance and we are the particles within His body. *"Faith is the substance o things hoped for, the evidence of things not seen,"* according to Hebrews 11:1.

There is a Greek word for substance called *hupostasis,* which means a setting under, support or person. Christ is the reality or structure that underlies all outward manifestations and change—He is the person the hupostasis talks about. Also, in Hebrews 1:3, He is all that upholds all things by the word of His power. Instructional mentoring without a structural life produces leaders with good instruction but no structure. Structure is important because it is the foundation upon which everything else stands. I have witnessed people who have good teaching ability but certain portions of their lives have no structure. Torment destroys structure. Structure also means keeping your priorities together. You can tell a person that has structure because they have their priorities together. They have aligned and structured their lives according to the Kingdom.

Mentors who have aligned and structured their lives according to the Kingdom have a greater chance of mentoring than tormenting. An unstructured life is a life headed for destruction and in the process destroying every other life they come in contact with. Most people who do not have structure were not taught it, became adjusted their way of life, and do not feel it is a necessary element. I believe more people want instruction than they want structure. I may be wrong, but that is my observation. I have observed more people getting what they want instead of what they need; but all the knowledge in the world cannot hold a marriage, family, ministry, business or any other relationship together. They all need structure or a good foundation. Foundation is just another word for structure. I believe failure is produced because there is either no structure or foundation, or the wrong structure is present. Kingdom structure is rejected in this generation.

The time is now to produce mentors that have Kingdom structure— time to tear down again the high places that the Manassehs of this age have rebuilt. A person may very well have had some good structure, but because of a bad experience that structure was torn down. Just think for a moment about all the wrong perceptions that one may have because of the wrong structure. When I listen to what some think about various extreme issues, it really bothers me. In this compromising age, where homosexuality is taught in some churches as an alternate lifestyle by pastors, this structure wrong, and is the beginning of some boy child becoming confused and coming into an acceptance that being a homosexual is okay. Scripture clearly teaches us that it is an abomination. I use that as my example because many Christians are coming to accept the perception that this perverse lifestyle is right.

There are yet still many other structural perceptions that lay false or corrupt foundations that tend to lead to torment. Foundation and structure are everything, for they are the strength to all things. Another element that this generation is lacking is the ability to repair broken and torn lives. There is a great need for endurance and strength. I am a firm believer that just because an individual has authority does not means he has strength. Authority calls for instant response, but strength is the quality or state of being strong. It's a capacity for exertion or endurance. Strength means you have the power to resist; it's solidity and toughness that lasts. I want to say that when a person has strength, they have power to resist attacks.

I am reminded of a story in Judges about a man named Samson. He was the strongest man of his time, and everyone tried to figure out where his strength came from. I believe he didn't know where his own strength came from. In Judges 16:5-7 it says:

And the lords of the Philistines came up unto her (Delilah), and said unto her, Entice him, and see wherein his great strength lay, and by what means we may prevail against him, that we may bind him to afflict him; and we will give thee every one of us eleven hundred pieces of silver. And Delilah said to Samson, Tell me, I pray thee, wherein thy great strength lay, and wherewith you might be bound to afflict thee. And Samson said unto her, If they bind me with seven green withs that were never dried, then shall I be weak, and be as another man.

Samson played this deceitful game with her until he finally gave in and told where he thought his great strength lay. As many of us taught and preached at one point that Samson's strength was in his hair, I believe Samson's strength was never in his hair. I also believe the reason why his strength left is because God had to teach him the true source of his strength. Because as you continue to read his story, his hair began to grow back, but even then his strength was not replenished. It's not until Samson called unto the Lord and said, *"O Lord God, remember me, I pray thee, and strengthen me, I pray thee, only this once O God, that I may be at once avenged of the Philistines for my two eyes"* (Judges 15 and 16).

This generation of mentors and up and coming mentors, suffers from this Samson syndrome. Signs of this are observed in people who:
1) Are self-reliant upon their own strength or ability.
2) Begin to tempt God and because He is not the true source of their strength, they end up victims of their own deceitful schisms.
3) Have no clue to the true source of their strength.

My early years of the pastoral call began with what I thought was great success, because I planted a fresh work and had a few resources. I planted it next to an adult video store, in a building that was getting ready to get on the city's demolition list. About seven family members and I started having service in the building after I and my hired help—most of which were wine heads and drug addicts—filled up three eight foot by forty foot dumpsters, put a new roof on the building, and my friends Dr. David Lee Richardson from the Potter's house in Dallas, Texas, and Bishop St. John Lovelace from Toronto, tore down a major bearing wall, two stairwells, put up major beams, and opened the space up.

I'll never forget the labor it took for me and an elder who trained the first twelve elders of Bishop Jakes' church in West Virginia, and the Bishop who laid hands on me. I really learned early in ministry about true servanthood. Well, we began to have service in the building and the ministry was blooming quickly. I believe in the first two years we went from seven people to standing room only. Prayer was going on and at that time I met Pastor Tommy Reid. I told him that the Lord said the video store was going to close and we would have that building—and it happened.

It was a big deal to everyone but me. I did not see the significance at the time, but people were coming from everywhere. The service was anointed, and I had a staff of musicians, a worship team, a choir, and deacons. I mean everything that it would take people years to get, somehow just appeared to me. But, the ministry lacked structure and pretty soon God was not the source of my strength. I believed that the bragging and boasting that the people did about the anointing and the word in my mouth made me become self-reliant upon my own abilities. And because I forgot the true source of my strength, everything that God had built that I began to take credit for fell apart. I had been called the apostle of the region. Tommy Reid himself called me the set man, but because I began to depend on my own ability, I caught a great setback. My world quickly fell apart.

Empowerment Temple is again on the break in this city, only because I realized the true source of my strength. Even on a greater level, I am still responding to the call as one of the set persons in this region. I shared that because a Kingdom individual who does not see God as his or her only source loses their resources. For what we are called to do takes a greater strength that is beyond human ability; and our strength cannot be of our own or anyone else's but God the Father's.

The Samson's of this generation need to know the true source of their strength before they end up on Delilah's lap, deceived and helpless, or strengthless between two pillars. We have to produce a generation that trusts God to help them go the distance. When God becomes the source of strength, there are no words such as, "I am burnt out" or "I cannot go the distance." This generation of mentors need strength to stand against the wiles of the devil, it needs strength against divers temptations. This generation of mentors needs the strength to endure trials and tribulations, pain and suffering. I really don't mean to sound like I am preaching, but I feel the anointing of the Holy Spirit. Isaiah 40:28-31 says:

> *Hast thou not known? hast thou not heard, that the everlasting God, the LORD, the Creator of the ends of the earth, faint not, neither is weary? there is no searching of his understanding. He giveth power to the faint; and to them that have no might he increase* strength. *Even the youths shall faint and be weary, and the young men shall utterly fall: But they that wait upon the Lord shall renew their strength; they shall mount up with wings as eagles; they shall run, and not be weary; and they shall walk, and not faint.*

Habakkuk 3:19 says, *"The Lord God is my strength, and he will make my feet like hinds' feet, and he will make me to walk upon mine high places."* Just this right here should strengthen your hand. Samson played tricks and games with his gift and anointing. It's the same thing that Satan tries to do—he tries to trick Jesus in Matthew 4:5-7, tempting God. If I could have talked to Samson back then, I would have told him that he was playing with fire; and if you really don't know the true source of your strength, stay away from Delilah.

Can I speak to you prophetically for a moment? As I am typing on my computer and I feel an unction in my spirit to say this to you. Luke 22:31-32 says, *"And the Lord said, Simon, Simon, behold, Satan hath desired to have you, that he may sift you as wheat. But I have prayed for thee, that thy faith fail not: and when thou art converted, strengthen thy brethren."* This was not a word to Peter because he was not converted: the Lord spoke this to Peter because he knew that Peter would deny Him—He knew that fear would draw him back. When the Lord spoke to him and said, *"When you are converted strengthen your brethren,"* He was speaking in relation to Peter's conversion from fear. He would be strengthened by the Holy Ghost, and strengthen his brethren with that which he also received. This experience happens in Acts 2, and after that we see Peter bold in the faith and strengthening his brethren.

You have been the Samson and the Peter, and this is a season now for you to strengthen your brethren, you understand the true nature and source of your strength and you also have overcome the fears, and now it's time that you give an impartation and strengthen the hands of your brethren. You know that thy God hath commanded thy strength: now cry out on behalf of your brethren *"Strengthen, O God, that which thou hast wrought for us, because now is this time right."*

Now there is a critical need for strength in this generation and not self-sufficient strength that is not enduring, but reliance upon God's strength. If we have not recovered and received strength from the Lord over your experiences, and your strength came from some other source, eventually it will wear off. Your devices and resources for strength and comfort are only temporal, they are going to run out, and when the dependability upon your own strength and ability wears off, in the words of the Christ you are good for nothing but to trodden under the feet of man.

You are called "The restorer of streets to dwell in." This speaks volumes to me and you, because our city streets are not safe to dwell in because many have either turned from God or many never received Him. This generation of mentors is like a modern day savior operating off the strength and ability of our God, restoring the city streets and bringing salvation. Salvation means a deliverer or a preserver; one who saves from danger or destruction and brings into a state of prosperity and happiness; a rescuer. Being a mentor these days means that you are to rescue this generation. This generation is in serious need of salvation. Our city streets are dominated and controlled by drugs and gang violence, sex and disease, murder, hatred, porn, rape, child molestation, child abuse, and runaways—you name it, our city streets have it. Most people are contained in their own homes, afraid to go outside the safety perimeters they have set for themselves for fear of being a victim of the circumstances that plague our city streets.

These times call for a reformer. I am still speaking to you prophetically, so you can understand the seriousness of your call. You are called the restorer of the streets to dwell in. A *restorer* is one who turns back, returns, goes back; reestablishes, to take, to bring back, etc. There are so many applications for this word, but to sum it up, duty calls. And this duty requires individuals who are more concerned about the Kingdom's present and future mentors than they are about how popular and great they become.

This generation should not be more concerned about church protocol than they are about the call of God. Salvation will never reach our city streets until you take it there. You are God's final solution—you are the voice in the earth in these last times—your voice is to deliver and rescue this generation from the jaws of Satan.

I have lived in Buffalo, New York, all my life, and every year it seems as though our city streets wax worse and worse. I have finally come to the conclusion that our politics, government and law enforcement cannot fix the problem, because it's bigger than arrests, judges, and prison. Those are only momentarily solutions for an eternal problem. While those who sit in prison only think of a better way to do and get away with crimes, there is another generation picking up where they left off. Our city streets will not become safe again until we who know the power of our God go out and make a difference. They will not be safe until the Ezras and Nehemiahs of our time begin to bring spiritual renewal, restore the worship of our God back to Him, start repairing the walls and gates of our city, and push back Satan's power.

> *For the moth shall eat them up like a garment and the worm shall eat them like wool: but my righteousness shall be forever, and my salvation from generation to generation. Awake, Awake put on strength, O army of the Lord, my righteousness is near; my salvation is gone forth and mine arms shall judge the people; the isles shall wait upon me, and on mine arm shall they trust. For Zion's sake will I not hold my peace, and for Jerusalem's sake I will not rest, until the righteousness thereof go forth as brightness, and salvation thereof as a lamp that burns, and the Gentiles shall see thy righteousness .—Isaiah Chapters 59, 62*

This generation does not know what they need, because they were never taught what they needed. However, this generation of mentors that God Himself is preparing, knows what they need because the Father has revealed it to those who are seeking after His heart: proper structure, strength that is dependent on God, and salvation. This generation needs salvation and they need to see the righteousness of God in you! Our cities are filled with youth, Christians and non-Christians who are looking for mentors;

THE CRY OF A GENERATION:
Giving Generations What They Need

someone to help guide and push them into fulfilling their purpose. If the righteous are not willing to advise, teach, and coach this generation that is searching for direction, our children, our children's children, and our children's children, children will continue to produce a generation of torn-mentors, who will tear lives apart. This generation needs Jesus Christ; He is its greatest asset. They have been presented everything from religion, dollars in exchange for gifts, position, power and prestige, but they have not been given Christ. He is the only solution to true change and transformation, healing and wholeness. Anything else just covers and camouflages.

When people do not know who they are or their purpose for existing, they look for someone or something to model themselves after.

If we continue to mentor and give generations what they want or what we want to give them, we will continue to neglect the inner crying of their hearts that say, "We want a true leader." When people do not know who they are or their purpose for existing, they look for someone or something to model themselves after.

They create some superficial character to help them bring some kind of comfort to that inner longing for identity. For, some go through multiple characters, and then suffer from multiple personalities. You've seen them around running from one gift to the other—one minute they are a worship leader, then they want to preach the gospel, from there they want to be the choir director, then an adjutant. They go from one extreme to the next. They then want to be over the evangelism team. Because they are confused and powerless and did not have a mentor that gave them what they needed, they began to mix and mingle with the secularists.

Secularists are quick to make them feel accepted and comfortable—quick to show them how to do it, struggling from the Cain syndrome (that is, show me how to be accepted, I want respect too, show me how to do it, will someone show me!). This is why Cain got angry, because his brother refused to show him how to get respect and be accepted. But when someone is at the crossroads between two lifestyles, they will eventually cross over. This is the main reason why we cannot seem to convert those who have not been converted yet, because those who are converted end up being converted into their world. It goes back to a saying of mine: "What good can you tell someone about life in Christ, when your life is a crisis."

The reason I am saying all of this is because it all points back to the mentor who did not get what he or she needed, who gave those they mentored what they wanted and not what they needed, just so they can say they are producing. When you as a natural parent always give your children what they want and not what they need there is still a longing in that child for what he or she needs. If you

THE CRY OF A GENERATION:
Giving Generations What They Need

are a parent that gives materially and not affectionately, your child will have their material needs comforted by you and their longing for affection met by cousin Boe, Aunt May, the boy next door, the girl down the street, the teacher or whoever that source may be. Your child would be more excited about being around the individual who loves on them and hugs them most—whoever quenches that inner longing for love and affection. They would ask you for money and then go ask the person who shows them that affection to take them to the store.

Well, it's no different when you are mentoring. If you only continue to give individuals what they want and not what they need, there is still going to be that inner longing for fulfillment, and it does not make a difference whether it's right or wrong, as long as the longing is comforted. In the unlearned mind there in no connection to right or wrong, only the awareness of comfort and discomfort. Even though in the eyes of the beholder it looks right, and we know it's wrong, to them it only feels right.

The need for this generation only seems greater than any other generation because the number has increased. Now, instead of being one or two generations behind, we are about three or four—maybe even more. Mentoring these days is very challenging right now, because so many wants have been portrayed as needs. But God has given us His ability. Listen to me closely, if you never had a mentor, or have been waiting for someone to come and mentor you, you need to shift your focus and put your attention on Jesus Christ.

The truth is that some of us will never get what we need waiting and depending on man to give it to us. Your life is passing you by while you wait on someone to come and lay hands on you and tell you who you are and what your purpose is. This generation is dying in need, and the worst way to die is to never have your need met. We cannot afford to have another generation die off without Christ, He is the need.

There is a work that God wants to perfect in your life, but it starts with you and Him first. He wants to download Himself inside of you and produce Himself in you, so that everyone that you come into contact with you can reproduce the character and personality of Jesus Christ in them. Isaiah 58:12 states, *"And they that shall be of thee shall build the old waste places: thou shalt raise up the foundations of many generations; and thou shalt be called, The repairer of the breach, The restorer of paths to dwell in."* There is no time for you to waste, great mentor—there is a generation that needs you to give them an impartation.

When those who have been without all their lives get an opportunity to give, they have a tendency to give what they always longed for and never got, because they know how it feels to be without. It's these individuals that God will use in this last time to help prepare a people. These people are like me and you. I just pray right now in Jesus' name that God our Father will give you the strength to respond and fulfill all that He has called you to, and that all that has happened to you in your past is broken off you. I pray that the Kingdom of our God will invade your mind, shift your heart, and position you to be the forerunner for the Lord's final appearance. This I pray in Jesus' name, AMEN.

Chapter Eight

Be Careful "Who" You Chase

We have covered so much in the formal chapters and as I continue to write, I am getting sensitive to the Holy Ghost because I am remembering the experiences that I had on this Christian journey. I remember how He covered, protected, and brought me out. As we spoke about earlier, the wants and desires for mentors are at an all-time high. In these times, there is such desperation for a physical manifestation of a mentor that most people neglect the very need of Christ and forfeit His leading and guiding in exchange for a man or woman who is in need of the same thing.

This can send the desperate on a chase. This can cause individuals to begin to be tossed to and fro, seeking out someone that can advise, teach and coach them into purpose. The danger of this is that you become so desperate in your pursuit that *everybody but the right somebody* becomes a potential candidate, and in such perilous times like these without proper direction from God and prayer, you will try to push and force yourself on someone who neither has the time or anointing.

Lawrence J. Moore, Jr.

I remember growing up at home; my life to me was kind of strange. To me, as I got older, it did not seem normal, because I grew up around girls and women. My father was not around. I don't even have precious memories of a father or mentor. I enjoyed playing with my sisters, I mean we come from a large family of six girls and five boys. I fell number six in line after five sisters, so jumping jacks, double-dutch, paper dolls, and Barbie and Ken dolls were play time for me. I was not into sports and even now, I am not interested. Now that might sound funny to some men and I'll watch a football game or basketball every now and then, just for the brethren's sake, but I don't get excited over who wins or loses.

As I grew up, I did not feel right. I was picked on because I was passive. One guy use to chase me and all my little brothers home, and there was nothing I could do about it—well at least that's what I thought. One day, I saw the guy beating and bullying one of my younger brothers and for the first time I knew I had to help him. I fought him and won. I believe that even though I won, it was the worst thing that could happen to me because winning proved to me that I could fight. I began to get into trouble in school. I was suspended and kicked out of every school I went to, because I became a thief, bully, and extortionist. I was sent to an all-boys school, and from there I got a final shot at a regular school—which did not work.

The street life became my final solution, and by that time I was not looking for a father or mentor, I was looking for someone to show me the streets. Chasing behind the wrong people, I learned to be a burglar and a robber. From there I went from running with gangs, to drug dealing, to gun selling, which led to my conviction three different times for felonies. After doing time, not counting all the other multiple arrests, I knew I could fight and win, so I had no fear for the police. My mother watched as they beat me at police headquarters while I was cuffed. I was extremely aggressive but they could not hurt me. The more they hit me, the angrier I became. I even held a police officer at gun point one time. It was only the hand of God that kept me from being killed.

Then, early February of '97, the Lord saved me; and when the Lord saved me, I found myself on a chase, looking for someone to mentor me. I wanted to be a solid Christian. I did not want to do it alone because I did not want my spiritual life to end up in a shipwreck like my natural life. But, it seemed as though the only type of men that I would run across were lustful people who would call themselves prophets, and preach fire and brimstone in the church, but would preach another message to women behind closed doors. Others were either too dominating and controlling, too religious, or very traditional and powerless. Others were still dominated by sin and rebellion.

The ones that I wanted were the breed of men that I thought were blameless, and even though I heard rumors about some, my spirit would not allow me to believe the hearsay. To me they were so powerful and anointed, and had springing, thriving churches, but they did not have time for me. As much as I was interested in them, they were not interested in me. I started to believe that it could have been because I was not a church boy and that I did not have degrees in theology, nor attended seminary school, so that kind of hurt me. Every time I called, my calls would go unanswered for weeks or even months. I chased, chased, chased and chased, and it only ended up in pain and disappointment.

I am now in the seventh year of my pastoral call and as of yet, I have not found anyone that has really taken me into their bosom and fathered or mentored me. I have never had anyone who was consistent in advising, teaching and coaching me; and now being who I am, I can understand why in one sense—but then in another there is a question mark. On my journey to find a mentor, I have encountered at least four types in my chase:

1) THE PROJECT MANAGER
2) THE PROMISE-BREAKER
3) THE PROMOTER
4) THE INCONSISTENT COUNSELOR

My personal pursuit for a mentor has ended in me feeling rejected and disappointed. So in a sense, I felt like history was repeating itself. I had no one in my natural life and no one in my spiritual life. I began to accept the fact that God was doing something that was different. Men always feel they need to have someone *first* and then have God *second*. What God was doing with me was giving me a revelation about His nature *first*, so that when and if He sent me a mentor *second*, I would not have a problem identifying who it would be. So, after pursuits that led to no progress, I accepted God as my mentor and as He advises, teaches and coaches me through the Holy Spirit, His character and personality are being producing in me.

It is puzzling to me how we pursue and chase down men who are in need of what we need and trying to get something from them that they do not have to give or are struggling in areas just like us. Now I do have three or maybe about four great men in my life who from time to time give me some wisdom and advice—and teach and coach me on a natural level. But when it comes to giving me that inner, life-changing, mind renewing, heart and spirit transformation, they cannot give me that. After all, that comes from God, and as of yet, none of them have stepped up to really pour into my life on a mentor level.

I am a firm believer that sometimes God will rise up an individual and allow them to go through certain experiences that others do not have to experience—that they might benefit from the life and experience of that person. In my pursuit of chasing men, I almost missed God. I came so close to almost forfeiting the anointing on my life by depending on man to give me what only God could give. I was going through the toughest period I have ever gone through in my life.

I was married and a new pastor. The marriage was very rocky. The church was doing well, at least I thought it was. One year I was a speaker at a men's conference in Detroit. I was gone for three days. When I got home, my pregnant wife and three daughters were gone. The house was completely empty, and later on I found out she was living with another man and the child that I thought was mine was his. Without getting into a lot of detail, I was left feeling abandoned by both my family and church. Satan had made me feel that he really turned everyone against me. At this time I really was on a chase for someone to advise, teach and coach me through this most difficult period. But I found no one, I really felt alone. People whom I really thought had my best interest had no interest at all. I sat around confused and kept saying it was not my fault that it happened to me! I thought suicide was a way out, I mean my whole world went from having everything to feeling like I had nothing. I thought that someone I reached out to would eventually feel my pain and come and help rescue me. Due to fighting depression, I really did not have a desire to pastor the church anymore and it showed. I did not have a desire to pursue God any further and the church shifted. I was mentally, emotionally, and spiritually confused and torn. When you get to where I was, you have to be careful who you chase, because most people will unintentionally help push you right over the edge. I also realized that for some people, if they are not benefiting, you are not receiving.

In this chapter, I want to give you four individuals to stay away from in your pursuits. You must avoid them at any cost, because to chase them is a torment in itself. The first individual to watch out for is *"The Project Manager."* This individual never embraces you as a vessel to pour in to. He or she is more interested in things that you have that will benefit them. They see you more as a project than an object of purpose. A project is something that is a good, bright idea or specific plan or design; a task or problem. To a project manager, you are nothing more than a bright idea or a good old project. When the project manager thinks of you, it is at a board meeting with the rest of his or her staff. And it's only because you are an opportunity to better their project, so they will deal with you and make you feel a part of the team until their project is over. They will support your events and endeavors or pour into your life, but they will never deal with you on a personal, intimate or relational level. When you are viewed as a project, you are not associated with that particular body, but are viewed as an assignment, or some charity case. It's very disappointing when you think you are being mentored after you have chased and pursued an individual, only to find out their interest in you is not genuine. You were nothing more than a good idea. You need someone that is genuinely concerned about you as a person and is willing to give you themselves; not someone who just views you as a project or a profit. In these times, we are missing genuine mentors who really have a heart to embrace wholeheartedly those they mentor. Too many people are in the hustle and bustle of ministry and trying to build their own little empires. They are neglecting the true, needs of those who so desperately need them to advise, teach, and coach them. This generation does not need project managers, but true coverings.

The second individual you need to be aware of is *The Promise Breaker.* These individuals make promises that they never keep. They never follow through with agreed upon plans. I understand that sometimes we make promises and circumstances can prevent us from keeping our commitments but a promise breaker is consistent in breaking their commitments to you. I do believe that some people have intentions on advising, teaching and coaching you, because they see something in you that if molded correctly, can cause you to potentially grow into someone even greater than themselves. But then you have some who only make half-hearted attempts to advise, teach and coach. They set up appointments with you, but it is just a way of hurrying you along, because they never have any real intentions on meeting with you in the first place. When someone makes a commitment to spend time with you and it is broken, that means that you are not a priority and anyone that mentors you must see you as a priority. Your life is important to them.

If God assigns a person to you, they will follow through and follow up with you. You won't find yourself always chasing behind them, but they will call and see about you as well. It can be frustrating when there is urgency in your life and you really need some advice. Teaching or coaching plans are made to help counsel you through tough times when they are broken you are left feeling like you are not a concern. Mentors who have your best interest at heart will never intentionally break a promise or make one they cannot keep unless it is really beyond their control. Your destiny and purpose is a priority to them and they show it in words and action. To them you are not just a project or something to do. They understand that there is an impartation that must take place—transference of life. A mentor is a type of a mid-wife who is there to help prepare you and coach you through your birthing process. They refuse to leave your side until you have given birth to a healthy, well-nourished ministry. So time is of the essence—it is important to them, as a result they will not make promises that they cannot keep. They will make every effort to give you the time to advise, teach, and coach you. You have to be careful that you do not get caught chasing behind a "Promise Breaker" because they will break your heart, they will constantly let you down. *"The blessing of the LORD, it make rich, and he add no sorrow with it"* (Proverbs 10:22). People who constantly break promises in your life have no consideration for your well-being, and it is just their way of saying I don't have time—heed to the warning. The best thing they could have done is announce to you who they "really" are.

The *Promoter* is the mentor that is more interested in advising, teaching and coaching your gifts than he is in you. The promoter uses your gift for their personal gain. They will always be there, they will never leave or forsake your gift, they will never break promises. They are very consistent but only because there is a motive. He or she is driven by selfish intents, this mentor is a manipulator and deceiver, they will use your gift to pack out a meeting, to raise money, to put themselves in the limelight. When the promoter looks at you they see themselves, they do not even notice you. If given the opportunity, they will control and dominate your gift. The promoter sees you as a door of opportunity and if you allow their deceit to blind you, your encounter with them can be a very damaging experience. The promoter is nothing more than a pimp in the pulpit prostituting your gift and anointing. I have heard some horror stories from musicians, worship leaders, choir members, men and women of God with prophetic gifts or individuals who have served people that they thought were their mentors. They thought they had their best interests at heart; but they were nothing but promoters. As long as they could control who, what and where they used their gift, they got what they thought was genuine love.

The promoter will drain and burn you out if you allow them to, and when you are no good, they will look for someone else to replace you with—something fresh that has not been used up. The promoter is a wolf in sheep's clothing. His love is all about *Eros,* which is love that says as long as you give me what I want, I love you. At this point in my life, this is my observation: there is a lack of mentors because man, by nature, is a selfish being and everybody wants something for themselves until the Kingdom of God to invades their human nature. The promoter is out for self-gain, and if you chase and pursue this individual, you will be mentally, emotionally, and spiritually desolate. The worse thing a person can do to you is withdraw from you, but never have a deposit to give. Paul says in 2 Timothy 3:1-5, NCV:

> *Remember this! In the last days there will be many troubles, because people will love themselves, love money, brag, and be proud. They will say evil things against others and will not obey their parents or be thankful or be the kind of people God wants. They will not love others, will refuse to forgive, will gossip, and will not*

control themselves. They will be cruel, will hate what is good, will turn against their friends, and will do foolish things without thinking. They will be conceited, will love pleasure instead of God, and will act as if they serve God but will not have his power. Stay away from those people.

Paul here warns us about the people we should not let influence our lives. All the people he named in this text are driven by selfish intents or works of the flesh.

The last person I want to help you identify is the <u>Inconsistent Counselor.</u> In order for a person to really make an impact in your life, there has to be some consistency. You cannot help advise, teach or coach a person one hour every few months. There has to be an established relationship. Too many times, we find ourselves consistently pursuing our mentors, or individuals we want to mentor us, but they are not consistent in their response to us. The inconsistent counselor is sincere, yet the problem is his time is periodic. One reason could be there is no common ground. There are differences that divide—it can be cultural, religious, or social. They feel as though they need to relate to your culture, religion, or social status before they can make themselves available to the capacity where they are spending quality time with you. Culture, religion or social status should not stand in the way of showing someone the same consistency you would if they were the same race, religion, or spoke as intelligently as you. If the inconsistent counselor looks past all the human dynamics about mentoring, there will be some stability in his availability.

Too many times, we cut ourselves short chasing behind individuals who are just tolerating us or who really do not have our best interests at heart. When you are interested in someone mentoring you but you start feeling more like a project or they seem to be more interest in your gift than you, that is probably not the correct mentor for you. When you sense wrong motives and intents, or whenever you find someone that is always breaking appointments and promises, and showing inconsistency, that should be a red flag for you to drawback and pray about it.

Chasing behind anyone for any reason at all is putting yourself in harm's way. Many people have been hurt because of rejection, many have taken the offensive, stating that they desired a particular person to mentor them and their cry was ignored. Just know that everyone you are interested in is not interested in you or may not be who God has for that assignment in your life. Putting complete trust and confidence in someone that has the same potential as you have to disappointment someone is too much control for a man or woman to have over another.

From time to time, I wish that I could call on someone and have a sit down, to let it all out. A talk with someone that understands. A physical figure that can relate to my hurts, struggles, fears, failures, disappointments, and that can give me an answer that will help me get through what it is that I need to get through. Sometimes we feel that if we had someone to advise us not just through our successes but through our struggles as well, and that would teach us—

pointing, coaching, and steering us in the right direction, we believe it would help condition our minds and hearts in the flesh. We believe our lives would be alright. This is the issue we face: we just want to be filled so that we can fulfill, but what we fail to realize is that the part of us that needs to be filled cannot be filled by man.

I do not care how many mentors you chase and how many words they speak to you, there is going to always be a void. There is a longing for righteousness in us that needs to be filled—a void that no man can fill. In Matthew 5:6, Jesus says: *"Blessed are they which do hunger and thirst after righteousness: for they shall be filled."* The word <u>after</u> means in its original content "to pursue." It's legal for me to say chase. So, if we are to be in pursuit or in a chase, it should be for the righteousness of God. This can only be accomplished through Jesus Christ, the greatest Mentor ever, which we will cover in our next chapter.

Our pursuits should not end in disappointment, rejection, pain, regret, bitterness, or feeling that we have been pimped. They should not leave us feeling drained and burnt out, but they should leave us feeling fulfilled, whole and complete, replenished and revived, like we are on the road of destiny and purpose.

As I said in a previous chapter it is dangerous for us to be attracted and drawn to someone else's anointing to the point where we start pursuing and chasing them down. You can chase something that looks and sounds good publicly, but privately they have neither the attributes nor the character that God wants to produce in you. The dominate anointing is the anointing of Jesus Christ; that's the true rich apostolic anointing—not the Jesus only of the apostolic faith. Isaiah 61:1-4 says:

> *The Spirit of the Lord God is upon me; because the Lord hath anointed me to preach good tidings unto the meek; he hath sent me to bind up the brokenhearted, to proclaim liberty to the captives, and the opening of the prison to them that are bound. To proclaim the acceptable year of the Lord, and the day of vengeance of our God; to comfort all that mourn. To appoint unto them that mourn in Zion, to give unto them beauty for ashes, the oil of joy for mourning, the garment of praise for the spirit of heaviness; that they might be called trees of righteousness, the planting of the Lord, that he might be glorified. And they shall build the old wastes, they shall raise up the former desolations, and they shall repair the waste cities, the desolations of many generations.*

This scripture speaks volumes! This is some of the work of that anointing. This is what we should be in pursuit of. This is what we should be chasing. There is no risk involved here, of any heartache or disappointment; maybe some trying of the faith, but that is for growth purposes only. We should find ourselves chasing God through Jesus Christ for advice, teaching and coaching, looking to Him who is the author and finisher of our faith (Hebrews 12:2). I have a saying that it took some time for even me to follow, that is

"For fulfillment seek after Jesus Christ, and for failure seek after man." As I come to a close in this chapter, there is nothing wrong with sitting in someone's office and having a face-to-face with those who really have care and concern for your well-being. But when you reach the point where you are totally dependent on them and you cannot do anything unless they are telling you what to do, that is a dangerous situation for any man or woman to be in. You will forfeit everything that Christ has accomplished for you!

This is what I believe: man has in a sense failed God when it comes to preparing generations for Kingdom business, and I believe God is doing a work in our lives through the Holy Spirit that man cannot take credit for. When we as humans, put our complete trust in another human that has the potential to be the worse choice in the world—we are setting ourselves up for hurt and disappointment.

Let me clarify what I am saying so it will not be said that this book has produced a generation of rebels. I say that jokingly, but if this book has caused you to rebel against man and submit in complete obedience to God, and be more concerned about His Kingdom, then I have done what I was sent out to do to shift you. By no means am I saying cut off your fathers and mentors in the faith. No! You should continue in their counsel if their counsel and mentoring points you to Christ; but do not chase them, chase God. Remember the words of the wisest man alive, King Solomon: *"There are many devices in a man's heart; nevertheless the counsel of the Lord, that shall stand"* (Proverbs 19:21). There are so many different devices a man can counsel you by. Devices are plans, procedures or techniques. Here it means a scheme to deceive, throughout this chapter you heard a few out of the hundreds of devices that are in a man's heart designed to cause you to lose sight of the one you must stay focused on. There are many different motives and reasons why men do as they do, but those devices will dig ditches, pits, and bury you in them. The counsel of the Lord shall kept you standing.

I cannot say it enough, everyone you want does not always want you, and everyone you desire does not always desire you. And if they do, you need to make sure that their motives and intents are pure. Some pursuits and chases have led some individuals into backslidden conditions, while others are dying in their pursuits. You have to realize that what God wants to accomplish and do through you, Satan wants to demolish in you, and it is so much greater than what you are chasing. I leave you in this chapter with this thought: look at what you are chasing in man and what man has to offer, and look at all that Jesus Christ offers in your pursuit after Him. Then ask yourself, "What have I gained in my pursuit in man forsaking Christ?" Your answer will be nothing. Now ask yourself, "What will I gain in pursuing Christ forsaking man?" You answer will be the Kingdom, both the now and the not yet. Weigh your options and then ask yourself, "What is more beneficial to my life?" When you look at man, and try to compare him to Christ, there is no comparison. Now choose ye this day whom ye will serve!

THE CRY OF A GENERATION:
Be Careful "Who" You Chase

Chapter Nine
The Great Mentor

When it comes to mentors, we have read about some good examples. There was Moses for Joshua, Eli for Samuel, Naomi for Ruth, Elijah for Elisha, and Paul for Timothy. I am pretty sure that there are more, but even though these mentors were good for those they mentored, my thought is still that man can only take you so far. Man's work is limited because our natures are carnal. Jesus is the greatest mentor that ever lived, He is the Great Mentor! He was and still is the greatest advisor, teacher and coach that men have ever beheld. What greater honor can one have than Mr. Destiny Himself as an advisor, He was the ultimate counselor. As a teacher, He gave direction that no man could touch—He was on point and accurate, for He pointed those He mentored. He was the figure and portrait for direction; and as a coach, He guided their mental and moral development, preparing the minds of those He coached for the things to come. It's called mental conditioning. Jesus the man, not the Christ who rose from the dead, was the greatest mentor ever, because He mentored towards the direction of righteousness in God—He was that righteousness.

The reason, I feel, that it was necessary to focus on Jesus the man before He died and rose as Christ our Lord, was because I believe His earthly work was mentoring. Even though He came to die and reconcile the world back to God, before that could happen He had to prepare and mentor men and women who He could download Himself into—men and women that can continue His earthly assignment while He moved on to the greater work, which was mediating and advocating for us.

Jesus *the man* advised, taught, and coached man what to do, but Jesus Christ our *Lord and Savior* empowered them to do it. Before we go any further, I would like to lay a foundation as to why He is the greatest mentor that ever lived and why He must be the one we seek for advice, teaching and coaching. One reason is because he is the fulfillment of everything God intended for man to be in creation. He points us right back in the direction of God's original plans and purposes for man before the fall in Eden. Isaiah 11:2-3 says:

> *And the spirit of the Lord shall rest upon him, the spirit of wisdom and understanding, the spirit of counsel and might, the spirit of knowledge and of the fear of the Lord. And shall make him of quick understanding in the fear of the Lord: and he shall not judge after the sight of his eyes, neither reprove after the hearing of his ears:*

Jesus is the mark for us all. Now, let's keep in mind that mentoring is the transference of life from one vessel to the other, through advising, teaching and coaching; and in this case, it is the life of the Holy Spirit, which is Jesus Christ's life, character and personality. Isaiah 11:2-3 speaks about the type of spirit that Jesus at His appearance will operate in; and it is also the same spirit that He imparts into us earthen vessels. After His resurrection and ascension, He is able to download Himself into the lives of those He mentored when He walked the earth.

This impartation of life will be the substance and power that causes the character and conduct of one's life to align itself with God's standards. This is evident in the lives of some of the men that He advised, taught and coached when He walked the earth, those who received an impartation of His spirit, life and character. For instances- there's Peter who was a doubled-minded, brawler, and ear chopper, before being mentored by Jesus he reacted on human impulses and instincts instead of logical reasoning. But after moving from fear to faith and receiving the Holy Spirit—the life, character and personality of Jesus Christ—on that great day of Pentecost, he became a pioneer of the established New Testament Church.

Peter became that rock upon which the Lord established His church...of which the gates of Hell would not prevail against. Peter whose character and conduct was at one point out of alignment, now teaches believers about both their character and conduct; how that it must be above reproach, and how being born again into a living hope is to imitate Christ and not to be an imitation. Nothing that man could have said or done to Peter would have given him that life-changing experience that he had after being advised, taught and coached by Jesus and filled with the Lord's spirit. Another example can be found in the lives of brothers James and John, the sons of Zebedee, were driven by position, power, and prestige. They were dominated by selfish ambitions before being advised, taught and coached by Jesus, and converted and filled with the Lord's spirit during the upper room experience. It was James and John who were more concerned about a position than about Jesus' life after He told them He was going to Jerusalem to die. It was James and John who ran to Jesus, looking for praise after they had street evangelism and informed Him that there was a certain man that had been casting out devils in Jesus' name. James and John forbid the man to do this because he was not a part of their clique. Instead of praise they got rebuked. It was James and John who started the argument among the disciples about who was the greatest. It was James and John who did not even want children to get close to Jesus because they thought they would get what they wanted (Mark 9:33-34, 10:37, Luke 9:49, Matthew 19:14).

But after being mentored by Jesus and having His life, spirit and character downloaded into their lives, all throughout the Epistle of James; he talks about faith and works—works being that of obedience. James talks about faith and works towards his fellowman. His whole epistle deals with how you treat other people; and John in his epistle, talks about love and fellowship with God. I have not heard anyone talk about love the way he speaks about love. He sounds like his mentor Jesus! These are just a couple of testimonies of those who have been advised, taught and coached by the Great Mentor Himself. Finally, I must speak about Saul, who had all types of degrees that he achieved as a Pharisee and at one time pursued and killed followers of Christ. But after having a spiritual encounter with Jesus Christ the risen Lord, his character, conduct and personality completely shifted. Saul become Paul and was willing to forget all that he learned prior to Christ. Paul received fresh advice, teaching, coaching, and even a name change from Christ.

We see firsthand into the lives of believers the work of this great mentor. Throughout His whole earthly ministry, we see His love, concern and compassion for the people He was called to produce change in. This great mentor was on a mission, and His mission was to change mankind. He would not stop. There was nothing anyone could say or do to prevent Him from having an impact on humanity. He was God's purpose and destiny, preparing people to fulfill His own destiny. The Great Mentor, Jesus, gives His life to and for those He mentored. Another reason why He was the Great Mentor is because He served. You cannot give yourself without servanthood.

Sadly, many mentors in our day and time have lost their ability to serve, or never were advised, taught or coached to serve. Jesus, the Great Mentor, said something that He demonstrated more in actions than in words. In Matthew 23:11 he says: *"But he that is greatest among you shall be your servant."* This is just another reason why He is the Great Mentor, because he taught that greatness is characterized by serving, and sometimes serving means moving beyond human limitations. This means that you will have to look beyond faults, failures and human flaws. Don't just mentor me when I am doing well, but even when I want to cut off ears and brawl, or have the wrong perception, or struggle with sin—mentor me!

Jesus went beyond human limitations by being touched with the feelings of those He mentored. He, looked beyond infirmities, faults, sins and human frailties, not seeing them as a reason to withdraw and distance Himself. He used them as a reason to move towards them with compassion. Man, untouched by the feelings of one's infirmities, will look upon a person's faults and failures and use them as a means to distance himself; or as we say, to fallback. The Great Mentor used them as opportunities. Usually, the best times to win someone over is when everyone else is withdrawing from them. Jesus was an opportunist looking for an opportunity. He used a person's infirmity for moments to touch and mentor. For even in Matthew 4:23-25, 5:1-2 it says:

> *And Jesus went about all Galilee, teaching in their synagogues, and preaching the gospel of the kingdom, and healing all manner of sickness and all manner of disease among the people. And his fame went throughout all Syria: and they brought unto him all sick people that were taken with divers diseases and torments, and those which were possessed with devils, and those which were lunatic, and those that had the palsy; and he healed them. And there followed him great multitudes of people*

> *from Galilee, and from Decapolis, and from Jerusalem, and from Judaea, and from beyond Jordan. And seeing the multitudes, he went up into a mountain: and when he was set, his disciples came unto him.*
> *And he opened his mouth, and taught them, saying...*

(If you read the rest of Matthew 5:3-16 you will see what He taught them.) Jesus did not take advantage of this opportunity to glorify Himself or to boast; He seized this opportunity to advise, teach and coach His disciples on how to wear their C.A.P. (Character, Attitude, Personality). He mentored them on how to conduct themselves when people treat you with great respect. He said the greater they treat you the more humility you must show. All those flawed, sick and frail folks they brought to Jesus, and those who followed just because, Jesus mentored and demonstrated what ministry is really all about. Then He continued to demonstrate through His actions what humility looked like—what serving looked like from a Kingdom perspective. He advised, taught, and coached them.

I would like to take this opportunity to repeat something I said earlier, but I want to say it a little differently so it will not sound as if I am repeating myself. Do what you want to say first, before you say and do not do it. What made Jesus the greatest mentor ever is His life was action and demonstration; He was a living example of what He taught. My new model for mentoring is demonstration first and explanation second. We need to reverse the way some of us are used to teaching, advising, and coaching for the sake of this generation. They've heard too much talk already. It's time for someone to demonstrate Christ. Most of the people knew who Jesus was. They knew because they had already read and studied the prophecies about Him, so when He came on the scene and demonstrated what they had read, they really did not have a problem receiving who He was because His actions demonstrated what they read. He did not have to come on the scene boasting and bragging about who He was—His actions spoke louder than His words.

The only people who had an issue were the haters. Just an observation of mine: the true reason I believe that Jesus was the greatest mentor ever is because He was the total package. I mean not only was He an advisor, teacher and coach, but He was also a deliverer, healer, comforter and redeemer—He was salvation. He was the fulfillment of all things. Not only did Jesus have the capability of advising, teaching and coaching those He mentored in the direction of the Kingdom of God and the fulfilling of the Kingdom assignment that was on their lives. He had and still has the ability to heal from any former hurts or pains that have left scars on our hearts. He even heals from emotional and mental pain and confusion. Jesus can deliver us from spiritual bondage; He is the restorer of your whole, entire man. What mentor have you ever encountered that can bring comfort to your mind, body, and soul? What mentor have you ever encountered that could speak one word in your life that could completely shift your world around? There are no limits nor boundaries to His activity in your life, as He quotes in Luke 4:18-19:

The Spirit of the Lord is upon me, because he hath anointed me to preach the gospel to the poor; he hath sent me to heal the brokenhearted, to preach deliverance to the captives, and recovering of sight to the blind, to set at liberty them that are bruised. To preach the acceptable year of the Lord.

His operation in our lives is universal, the only limits and boundaries that prevent Him from fulfilling his purpose in our lives are the ones we put up. He gets in areas that are impossible for any man to reach. When Jesus died to His own desires and then died on two wooden planks bearing His cross, He opened a pathway that could penetrate man's thoughts and heart. You and I could have never done what Jesus did. It's hard to do it now with Him living inside us. Men's ways are selfish even though we would like for people to think of us otherwise, but I have not run across one man who has reached the point where his life did not matter and everything he did was for the benefit of someone else. Jesus died to His own humanity to make sure that we all get what we need to get, or should I say it like this: so that we can have access to the Father and His Kingdom.

I believe that what makes a person a great advisor, teacher and coach is dying and overcoming their own pain and brokenness. As a matter of fact, it is very relevant that we do because those pains and hurts are the very things that God uses to train and equip us. Greatness is not determined by how much money or popularity you have—it's not determined by how well dressed or how many bedrooms and baths you have in your home—neither is it determined by what college you graduated from or number of degrees you have. According to secular standards, this is a false perception of what greatness is. Greatness is not even determined by your religious, social, or economic status. The Great Mentor said: "He that is greatest among you shall be your servant." Let me ask you a question: "How many people have you died for so that someone else can live?" I am not even talking about a physical death, but I am referring to a dying to your own desires. The Kingdom of God is a kingdom that is not driven on self: it is an unselfish kingdom.

The Great Mentor died twice as I stated in an earlier chapter. He not only died on the cross, but He also died to His own desires in the wilderness of "Temptation." I really believe that before God calls us to do anything, He calls us to die first. Jesus died to using what God gave Him for personal gain, He died to compromise, and He died to testing His faith by not being foolish. Then He died on the cross. The dying to self, made it possible to go the distance, even when His humanity wanted to resist the fulfillment of the cross.

Now let me shift for a moment. Jesus started mentoring men during His earthly ministry, and after He died and was resurrected from the tomb, He consummated that work. He was now able to go where no man had gone before. His resurrection made it possible for Him to plant Himself into our lives spiritually. Now He is advising, teaching, and coaching from down on the inside. How is that for a golden nugget! He started mentoring from an earthly perspective by demonstration and illustration, and when that time was fulfilled He shifted, and planted Himself inside of us to complete the work—and empowered us to do the same. He imparted His life, character and personality in us, and mentors us from the inside as we study His word. What an awesome work! He is not here physically like He was with Peter, James and John, but He left His word with us to enable us to do all that is written therein. He is the Great Mentor because he is the only mentor that deals with us from the inside out. Every other mentor you will encounter will probably start from the outside and may never reach you on the inside because man has never done what Jesus has done. The only thing man can try to do is get inside and penetrate your inner-being. Jesus *dwells* in your inner-being; He mentors and serves your intellect, advising, teaching, and coaching you through the Holy Spirit. From within He regenerates or rebirths our whole entire man.

I have come to realize a very important thing and that is, when it comes to my spiritual well-being, man is very limited. He can only take you so far in this walk. That is because man's nature is carnal. When it's all said and done, man's views and counsel is from an earthly perspective. Even if he does mentor from the word, his understanding of God's word is hindered by his own perception. And if his perspective is his own, his advice, teaching and coaching will only point you back into the direction of Christ anyhow. So why not seek Christ first for advice, teaching and counsel, and let Him lead you to man, just as he led Saul to Ananias (Acts 9). My intention is not to tell you to completely cut man off, but let Jesus Christ be your first and final source, and He will send a man if it is His desire for you to have one. Can I be honest? It is a waste of time for me to even want a spiritual impartation from man—because man has the potential to be as I am or even worse. Yes, physically man can validate me, lay hands on me, and cover me in the natural realm; but I need Jesus Christ to lay His hand on my inner man! The greatest impartation that you will ever receive will come from the Great Mentor Himself, not a man. The greatest advice, teaching, and coaching that you will ever receive will come from within. If you would just listen, God will use man to confirm what He already told you.

I love Bishop T. D. Jakes. I went to every Manpower conference there was. I drove from New York to Dallas alone, straight through, because I knew God had something for me there. Bishop Jakes laid hands on me and prophesied over my life and when I came home, I was never the same. That was only because he had spoken the Word of God over my life, and he spoke that which God had already told me. There was just no one in my home city of Buffalo who could or wanted to give it to me at the time, so I had to go all the way to Dallas to get it. But it was not Bishop Jakes' spirit and life that was transferred into me, it was the life of the word of God.

I love the ministries of Bishop Noel Jones, Benny Hinn and John Hagee; and I also thank God for Bishop Tommy Reid and Bishop

St. John Lovelace. These men have publicly declared the call of God on my life and spoken the word of God over me; but they can never give me what the Great Mentor provides me. It's not my desire to be like either of these men, I want to be like Jesus Christ. His anointing is the dominant anointing—it is because of His anointing that their anointing exist. I do not want someone to lay hands on my head, I want Jesus Christ to lay hands on my mind, thoughts, and heart. Man is limited by his nature. Yes, he can financially support you, open doors, and build platforms for you. And you can sit in his office behind closed doors and cry your little heart out, but there is a ministry beyond all of that, that is going to take more than you getting an open door at the Potter's House. You need to be touched by the life, character and personality of the Great Mentor to answer the cry in the earth from this generation for healing.

I spent my first six years in ministry feeling alone and abandoned, thinking that I did something wrong that I did not know about which caused people to distance themselves from me. I then realized that God was moving people away from me because He was moving Himself closer to me. One day I started to look back over my life and remember where I came from—all the way from my childhood until now. I sat down and wondered, how did I ever get to this point, because I did not have a father or mentor? I asked myself, how did my mind, heart, and spirit reach this place? How did my personality and character get to this place after years of running with gangs, drug selling, running guns and spending years in the pen? Even though I have a ways to go, where I came from was truly amazing. The Great Mentor began to speak to me and say that He was there all the time, advising, teaching, and coaching me from the inside. What I had been looking for He was already doing from the inside. I thought I needed to see a king, like Israel.

Most people who reject what God offers us through Christ for something they can see. I had the spirit and life of Christ living on the inside, and all it took was faith to believe that He could do an inside work in me by transforming me first before I used my faith to bring me material wealth. I could write another book about life, hurts, pains and sorrows, and how when I did not have a desire to be kept—when I felt like running away—He was there silently, without my awareness; advising, teaching and coaching me through the most difficult moments. Now the Great Mentor does work in the lives of other people, those who have themselves received His life and spirit, and become ambassadors for Christ—those whom God will use to advise, teach and coach you through His spirit. Isaiah 30:20-21 states:

> *And though the Lord give you the bread of adversity, and the water of affliction, yet shall not thy teachers be removed into a corner any more, but thine eyes shall see thy teachers. And thine ears shall hear a word behind thee, saying, This is the way, walk ye in it, when ye turn to the right hand, and when ye turn to the left.*

There are many times when the Great Mentor's advice, teaching and coaching will come from someone He spoke through in your life at some point or another. Did you not know that it was Him speaking? He will bring it to your remembrance—something that He told someone to tell you. Whether it was a pastor, mentor, teacher, mother, father, grandmother, friend, etc.—at the appointed time you will hear it.

Now again, I am not saying to cut off all those who are in your life that have been playing some part in making sure that you fulfill purpose. I am just saying that you need to know their limits, or if they are called to you at all. You cannot have complete confidence in flesh. As a matter of fact, have no confidence in it at all, because eventually they will die off and if that was your only source of advice, teaching or coaching you will be lost.

Moses died out of Joshua's life, Eli died out of Samuel's life, Naomi died out of Ruth's life, Elijah died out of Elisha's life and Paul died out of Timothy's life. Whoever is in your life will die as well, whether it's natural or spiritual death; but the Great Mentor will never die off—He lives forever throughout eternity. Our goal should be this: to be like Him. He is the purpose for our existence. So many people think that we were just created to live life and have fun; well that is true! But seriously, when God created man He created man with purpose: to be fruitful, multiply, replenish and subdue the earth, and to have dominion. Jesus, the Great Mentor, came to advise, to teach, and to coach us on how to carry out that Kingdom assignment. You are here to live your life fulfilling God's purpose.

Let me ask you question, just a little something to think about: "Do you think God would have created both you and me if Lucifer had never got expelled from Heaven?" Mmmmm, now that's something to think about, right? Spend your time on earth serving God's purpose and make every minute of your life count for something. Satan has horrifically shipwrecked lives and his plan is to get as many victims as he can to be sentenced to an eternity in Hell. Let the Great Mentor, Jesus Christ, advise, teach and coach you to fulfill your purpose here on earth; and to prepare this generation for the Lord's final coming.

Chapter 10
Ready for the Impartation

We have come to the final chapter of this assignment, and I can really feel a shift happening in my own life just releasing what the Holy Spirit birthed in me. And now, as forerunners for Christ's final coming, it is time for you to completely crossover. What I mean is that it is time for you to respond wholeheartedly to the Kingdom assignment that is on your life; it is time to rid yourself of former and past torments and hurts through complete obedience. You must surrender your complete man to the Great Mentor, Jesus Christ. Let his advice, teaching, and coaching bring comfort and help put some closure on your past. As he prepared the hearts and minds of his former disciples for the greatest move ever, let the Holy Spirit which is his life, character, and personality, impart the same power in you as well. I believe all of his teaching, coaching and advising is for the sole purpose of UN-hardening the heart of the believer; for they as well can receive this great gift of his presence.

I am reminded of a word of prophecy in Ezekiel 36:26 which says: *A new heart also will I give you, and a new spirit will I put with- in you: and I will take away the stony heart out of your flesh, and I will give you an heart of flesh. And I will put my spirit within you.* The impartation of His Holy Spirit, I believe, is to give us complete power and authority over the principalities, powers, rulers of darkness of this world and spiritual wickedness that wrestles with us in high places. These forces come to hinder our complete restoration and the work that we are called to do on the earth. It is impossible for us to effectively mentor men and women into discipleship in Jerusalem, Judea, Samaria, and the uttermost parts of the earth if we do not have power.

Mentoring and ministry will not be effective without His seal of approval. We can see the decaying of lives, leadership, people, and churches that do not have power. An illustration of His instructions are found in Luke 24:44-53, where Jesus told His disciples to preach repentance and remission of sins in His name to all nations. They themselves would be His witnesses, and He told them that He would send them a comforter, which is the promise of the Father. I believe this is the same prophecy in Ezekiel 36:26-27.

Jesus told His disciples to wait in Jerusalem until they have been endowed with power from on high and then departed after He blessed them. They worshipped and returned to Jerusalem with great joy and were continually in the temple, praising and blessing God. The disciples—moving from fear to faith, from doubt to belief—continued in that upper room with one accord in prayer and supplication. This generation has left Jerusalem before they received power. The ones that are still here have been inactive for too long to be effective. And there are probably those who never went at all. It's time for you to pray and give supplication in Jerusalem, and get endued with the Great Mentor's life, spirit, and power. One of our reasons for coming to church has been validated through the Great Mentor's words: "Wait in Jerusalem until you are endued with power from on high." Jerusalem is a place of worship, praise, prayer and supplication, not a place where we come to entertain and perform until we are burnt out.

There is no more time for talent shows, the hour is critical and the question you need to ask yourself is, are you ready for a blast of fresh air from His breathe? Are you ready for the Great Mentor's final impartation into your life? Most people's answer to that question would be yes; but then the question now becomes are you willing to do what it takes so that He can plant Himself in you, let His power work through you, and let His spirit direct you without you trying to apply His spirit and power where you want it? There is a surge of power that He wants to release into your life so that He can use you as a vehicle to drive Himself to and fro throughout the earth.

There is a great invitation known as a call that He sent you, and He has been waiting on a response from you. I know the battle between your present and your past is a rough one, but He wants to confront it and comfort you from it. Even though you are looking at yourself and saying what could Jesus possibly want with me—

He is saying I wish that you will make your mind up. He wants to use you—your pain, your torment, and your trials. Your wounds have relevance in His Kingdom. United with His word and power, you are the perfect solution for this generation. They need a mentor who has the Great Mentor's ability working through them.

Jesus Christ, the Great Mentor, needs your life and obedience so that He can continue His earthly work through you. He needs you to be transparent and not be afraid to show someone where you have been and who you are now. He needs to live on earth through your life, and there will be some necessary steps that you will have to take to receive this impartation, such as: let some people, places and things go; and get rid of habits that have been and will continue to hinder His work in your life. It is time that you take this moment in your life serious, it is time that you lay down every excuse that you used in the past as a reason why you should not—and use them for reasons why you should.

I am forty-two years old and I never had someone in my life that I could call a father or true mentor. I had a couple of mentors, but for years I felt disadvantaged and damaged because I never had a man to show me what manhood was all about. I had experienced manhood firsthand in my life, but I was ruined and I ruined others in the process. I never had anyone that wanted to come into my life and help me discover my true purpose or show me who I was Even when I was an associate minister, I did not feel like one because my pastor at the time was consumed with his own personal struggles and issues. As an ordained elder in the church, still did not feel like a minister because no one ever showed me how. Even though I received the Holy Ghost before my call, I did not feel like I had the power, so the silent cry in my heart was: *"Will someone please come along and show me something."* It felt like I was going to church just to have church. At my ordination as I sat on the front row and gazed up into the pulpit, seeing all the pastors, elders and bishops sitting up there looking dignified with their legs crossed, I knew in my heart that eventually if God didn't do something imperative for me I would become just like them, or I'd end up back on the streets. The feeling of being like them sent a chill through my spine and during the altar call, I cried out aloud because I wanted Jesus. I knew I was a Peter—I knew that I did not know how to love and treat women, or anyone else for that matter, because I had never been instructed on how a father, husband, or man treats people. Men, to me, were strong, dominating, had money, and at times were very arrogant. I was waiting for someone to start something with me because by this time, I was frustrated with everything. I started to pray but no one ever came. I started, however, to feel comfort, temperance, joy, peace, and love; and I was suffering long with the right attitude of caring about others—I knew I was changing.

A couple of months later my cousin was murdered, and that was it. I really needed someone because there was only one thing on my mind—revenge. I stopped going to church. I had one of my brothers and all my cousins with me one day. I had an AK-47 and a 45 caliber pistol, and we were riding, looking for the criminal that killed my cousin. We went to one club, and the brother of a friend of mine who is a pastor was the security guard for that club. He looked at me and said, "What are you doing here Elder Moore?" I said, "I am looking for someone." So I went in, but found no one. I dropped everyone off, and on my way home I drove up a street and saw some of the men responsible for my cousin's death. I tried to lift the AK-47 up to fire at the car they were in, but a force held that rifle down and I could not lift it.

I drove away with haste, got to the corner, pulled over and cried. I told my pastor about the incident. He slammed his hand on the desk and tormented me about being an elder, saying it is a shame before the church and that I should not feel that way. Eventually I went into someone else's office in city hall. They were able to speak life into my spirit and put me back in my right place. I got rid of the guns. I performed the eulogy at the my cousin's funeral. The Lord anointed me that day His glory filled that place so much so that during the altar call there was no more room for people to come. I came out of the pulpit with some of the other elders and we laid hands on the people. Many were saved and the Lord showed me that day who I was—I was called to win a lost and forgotten generation that the church had been unable to reach.

Please understand, this book was not written out of bitterness, resentment, or even to lash out at my tormentors, because I understand man. Religion is a totally different organization than Jesus and the Kingdom of God. This book was an assignment and I believe it was written to heal those who have been tormented, as well as to reveal my own struggles, to show my wounds, to let you know that you are not alone, and to testify of His great mentoring power. I share both your pain and struggle. God gave me this assignment to prepare and equip this generation that is sitting around in Jerusalem doing nothing, and those who have been in Jerusalem too long. I am called to help prepare them for their Kingdom assignments, and that means you.

When I was finally ready for my impartation from Christ, He did not hesitate to give it to me. I intentionally initiated some things and purposely set myself up to receive His life and power. One of the things I did was set my mind and heart according to God's timing, which meant I had to rid myself of the numeric and seasonal system that I allowed the church to put me on. I believed that God only showed up at certain numerical junctures or in certain seasons. When I felt like I had missed Him, I would come to church, not understanding that everything that God had to do He had already done and accomplished in Christ. Everything that pertained to my personal salvation was not still on a waiting period. It was fulfilled; so, that meant to me that at any given time or place I could get whatever I needed from God—whenever I made my mind up He was ready to give it to me.

So for us to continue to use excuses, such as "I am waiting on God" or "Please be patient with me, God is not finished with me," *"Thou art inexcusable, O man"* (Romans 2:1a). God is waiting on you, and you simply are not finished doing you yet. What God has done through Christ does not only confront the issues that torment you, but it comforts you as well. As bad as the Great Mentor wanted to stay, it was more to our benefit that He went away. Even the Mentor Himself says in John 16:7-8: *"Nevertheless I tell you the truth; It is expedient for you that I go away: for if I go not away, the Comforter will not come unto you; but if I depart, I will send him unto you."* The word <u>expedient</u> here means good or profit. The word <u>come</u> means to go with; adjuncts implying motion from one place to the other. An adjunct is something added or joined as an accompanying object, it means to assist. The word <u>comforter</u> means to be an advocate, counselor, or intercessor. What the Great Mentor is saying to you and I is that it is to our profit and benefit that He departs from the earth, because I cannot advocate from where I am on your behalf. There is something that I need to give you. As a matter of fact, I need to join or unite myself to you. I need to assist and accompany you from within, and if I don't go where I need to go, I cannot do that.

The Great Mentor's time for walking among the people was expired, it was now becoming time for him to live in us and to comfort us, so that we could be a comfort to all those we are called to mentor into discipleship. Paul says in 2 Corinthians 1:3-7:

> *Blessed be God, even the Father of our Lord Jesus Christ, the Father of mercies, and the God of all com- fort; who comforts us in all our tribulation, that we may be able to comfort them which are in any trouble, by the comfort wherewith we ourselves are comforted of God. For as the sufferings of Christ abound in us, so our consolation also abound by Christ. And whether we be afflicted, it is for*

THE CRY OF A GENERATION:
Ready for the Impartation

your consolation and salvation, which is effectual in the enduring of the same sufferings which we also suffer: or whether we be comforted, it is for your consolation and salvation. And our hope of you is stedfast, knowing, that as ye are partakers of the sufferings, so shall ye be also of the consolation.

This is why it was expedient for the Great Mentor to depart from the earth. We have tried every remedy from the counsel of man. We have tried walking into healing and comfort by just forgetting about it, which only lasts for a season. We have even tried to walk others into the same healing and comfort that we thought we had and found it was very unsuccessful. You cannot give someone something that you do not have yourself. When it is all said and done, true healing and comfort comes from the Comforter. If you are really serious about your Kingdom assignment and want to receive healing and comfort for your life and the lives around you, you need to receive this impartation.

Just imagine for a moment the lives and people that you will impact: family members, friends, co-workers, spouses, children, people in your community and city, people that you have been witnessing to for years. Receive the missing substance to do so. Isn't it about rescuing lives from the pain, hurt, and torment brought on by people who are where you use to be? How can you ignore the cry of this generation—the silent cries of the heart that are expressed through rape, murder, anger, bitterness, homosexuality, lesbianism, child molestation, abuse of women, child abuse, drug using, drug dealing, gang violence, etc. These are just a few manifestations of silent cries that express themselves through moral dysfunction. How can you continue to ignore the cry of your own heart for closure? These are issues that will continue to grow from bad to worse and from worse to catastrophic—potential torn and scorned mentors who will afflict on others the aftermath of the pain and torment they received.

We have already read who's doing it, what must happen, why it must stop, when it should stop, where it stops, and how it stops. If it has happened to you, you are probably doing it to others. It is you who must stop it! We have all, in some way, been tormented or have tormented others. What must first happen is healing needs to invade your heart and mind. Why? Because there are too many present and past generations that are hurting and need mentors after the Father's heart. When does it stops? Now! Where does it stop? With you! How must it stop? By receiving the impartation of the Holy Spirit that comforts and consoles; that heals, delivers and mends the broken hearted; that sets captives free—those in your home, church, community, city, schools, and jobs.

This anointing or impartation must hit the lives of every believer, because we have been called to impact and change the world. The world will not be changed unless we change it. It has to be a very hurtful feeling to God to know that the portion of creation that He called out to make a difference (the church) needs more change than the people they are trying to change. Some of us need to go back to Jerusalem.

It is my observation that believers are more guilty of tormenting and tearing lives apart than we are at making them better. I do not know how it is in your city, but our church traditions and religious systems have made the word of God of no affect. Position, power, and prestige have ruined and damaged lives. It is time for the believer to hunger and thirst after the righteousness of God so we can be endued with power from on high. This is the time and hour for complete submission and obedience to the will of God; it is time for you to shift from marinating in your torment to ceasing from it altogether. And if you are an individual who is chasing someone around who really does not have time to nourish and feed you, cease the chase and turn to the Great Mentor, Jesus Christ. Your rips and tears must be sown up, but your scars must remain visible. Your scars will be the very reason why you reap a great harvest for the Kingdom of God. Do not be ashamed or afraid to show where you've been.

This generation needs to see the wounded and scarred alive and well, mentoring with rips and tears on their head from mental torment —with scars on their hearts, hands, sides and feet that have been healed. This generation needs to see those who are mentoring from outside their pain and not from inside. This generation does not need to be mentored by individuals who are still bleeding and are dying, dragging themselves around on their last breath trying to find someone to sew their wounds up. They do not need people who are still nailed to their crosses in pain and agony, and still going through mental and emotional torment. They need someone who has died to carrying their cross, and to their own flesh and worldly desires. They need someone who now lives life through the resurrection power of the Great Mentor Himself, so that when they speak, it is as if the Lord Himself is speaking and breathing life into them.

Are you ready for the impartation? So many have forfeited this impartation through compromise. Every minute you spend on your cross contemplating whether you are going to get down or go the distance and tell the torment of your past it is finished, is another moment wasted and another person waiting. It is time for you to go the distance; there is a generation that is waiting to be touched by your life. People like you who are the forerunners for Christ's final coming are not an endangered species or the last of a dying breed; but you are the beginning of a new breed: the generation that will do the greater work. There is such a power in the atmosphere because of the need in the earth, and God wants to birth an end time move of the Holy Spirit that's going to be greater than any other move that any generation has ever experienced. The filling of the Great Mentor's spirit is the key element for the move and great harvest. You must begin to seek after the heart of God and let His voice speak through you. You are His final voice on the earth, you are His last words. Hebrews 1:1-3a NCV says:

> *In the past God spoke to our ancestors through the prophets many times and in many different ways. But now in these last days God has spoken to us through his Son. God has chosen his Son to own all things, and through*

him he made the world. The Son reflects the glory of God and shows exactly what God is like. He holds everything together with his powerful word.

In these last days God is still speaking to the world through His Son, who now lives in you; and it is the power of His word that is in you that holds everything together. Therefore, we that really believe His truth should want to be first partakers in this end-time filling of His spirit and move. It is time for you to receive the outpouring of His spirit so that He can speak through you and spread Himself from vessel to vessel. Someone is waiting. There are people that you are ordained to mentor into discipleship and fellowship with God— people that no one else will be able to reach.

How many times has someone spoken to you and their words fell on deaf ears, until one day the right person said something to you that made you shift and you responded quickly. When your world is turned around you must not hesitate in the moment of urgency, but you must move with haste. Again I say, there is such an urgency for you to seek the indwelling of the Holy Spirit so that you can become a healed, powerful vessel of the Lord. It's critical that we keep a firm grip on what we have heard so that we don't drift off. If the old message delivered by the angels was valid and nobody got away with anything, do you think we can risk neglecting this latest message, this magnificent salvation? First of all, it was delivered in person by the Master, then accurately passed onto us by those who heard it from him; all the while God was validating it with gifts through the Holy Spirit, using all sorts of signs and miracles as He sees fit. It won't happen without the life, spirit, and power of the Great Mentor Jesus Christ transferring Himself into your life.

With all that you are trying to do and accomplish in the Kingdom of God—the people whom you are trying to impact, and even your own personal issues and struggles—there will be no end to them, there will be no change until you invite Him in. Let Him become all that He has died to become in your life. Let Him reflect the image and likeness of the Father Himself through your life. Let Him change the world through you, starting with you. Even at this very moment if you begin to ask for it right now and become true and sincere in your petitioning, He will come in now and your life will never be the same. Let Him come to your rescue so that you can rescue lives. The world is depending and waiting on you; and they do not even know it. YOU are an extension of THE GREAT MENTOR.

Meet the Author

Pastor Lawrence J. Moore, Jr, is the founder and pastor of Empowerment Temple Kingdom Ministries, Inc., of Buffalo, New York. Currently providing leadership to this great house, Pastor Moore has not always walked in the charge of ministry. After a hard life of gang leading, drug dealing, and much time spent in "the big-house," the Lord served the pastor with a mandate and divine charge.

Pastor Moore is wreaking regional havoc on the enemy through the authority of a Kingdom message. With a heart inclined towards youth and the next generation, his commitment is to lead a "CAIN" generation into the place of Kingdom authority, through the establishment and implementation of youth crime prevention centers in every state of America. He has developed a mentoring curriculum called THE B.U.L.L.E.S. PROGRAM for young men and women, which is geared towards developing Character, Attitude and Personality (C.A.P.) for success in our present and future generation of young leaders. Lawrence has also established J.A.M. (Just Among Men). J.A.M. is a ministry for men to teach them how to build relational structure which, in turn, will help them maintain successful marital and family relationships.

Pastor Moore has studied at famed Elim Bible Institute, aspiring for a degree in Christian Ministry with a minor concentration in Marriage and Family and the Kingdom of God. Pastor Moore states that he himself, through God, has become a man of integrity and concern, and one who seeks and demands to "see" change. Proclaiming Matthew 5:1-16 as his model, he states: "I am perfecting to line up with the character and personality of the Kingdom. My life objective is to plant the original image and likeness of God back into humanity by preaching an uncompromised, Kingdom gospel, and a 'shifting' message until the Kingdom of God is manifested on earth and power returned to every believer! 'THE PLACE IS HERE—THE TIME IS NOW FOR THE SHIFT!'

www.ingramcontent.com/pod-product-compliance
Lightning Source LLC
LaVergne TN
LVHW051116080426
835510LV00018B/2075